Educational Leadership
and Louis Farrakhan

Critical Black Pedagogy in Education

Series Editor: Abul Pitre

The Critical Black Pedagogy in Education Series highlights issues related to the education of Black students. The series offers a wide range of scholarly research that is thought-provoking and stimulating. It is designed to enhance the knowledge and skills of pre-service teachers, practicing teachers, administrators, school board members, and higher education employees as well as those concerned with the plight of Black education. A wide range of topics from K–12 and higher education are covered in the series relative to Black education. The series is theoretically driven by constructs found in cultural studies, critical pedagogy, multicultural education, critical race theory, and critical white studies. It is hoped that the series will generate renewed activism to uproot the social injustices that impact Black students.

Titles in the Series

Educating African American Students: Foundation, Curriculum, and Experiences, edited by Abul Pitre, Esrom Pitre, Ruth Ray, and Twana Hilton-Pitre (2009)

African American Women Educators: A Critical Examination of Their Pedagogies, Education Ideas, and Activism from the Nineteenth to the Mid-Twentieth Century, edited by Karen A. Johnson, Abul Pitre, and Kenneth L. Johnson (2013)

Multicultural Education for Educational Leaders: Critical Race Theory and Antiracist Perspectives, by Abul Pitre, Tawannah Allen, and Esrom Pitre (2015)

Educational Leadership and Louis Farrakhan

Abul Pitre

ROWMAN & LITTLEFIELD
Lanham • Boulder • New York • London

Published by Rowman & Littlefield
A wholly owned subsidiary of The Rowman & Littlefield Publishing Group, Inc.
4501 Forbes Boulevard, Suite 200, Lanham, Maryland 20706
www.rowman.com

Unit A, Whitacre Mews, 26-34 Stannary Street, London SE11 4AB

Copyright © 2017 by Abul Pitre

All rights reserved. No part of this book may be reproduced in any form or by any electronic or mechanical means, including information storage and retrieval systems, without written permission from the publisher, except by a reviewer who may quote passages in a review.

British Library Cataloguing in Publication Information Available

Library of Congress Cataloging-in-Publication Data Available

ISBN 978-1-4758-3308-9 (cloth : alk. paper)
ISBN 978-1-4758-3309-6 (pbk. : alk. paper)
ISBN 978-1-4758-3310-2 (electronic)

∞ ™ The paper used in this publication meets the minimum requirements of American National Standard for Information Sciences Permanence of Paper for Printed Library Materials, ANSI/NISO Z39.48-1992.

Printed in the United States of America

Contents

Series Foreword — vii
Preface — xiii
Acknowledgments — xvii
Introduction — xix

1 The Purpose of Education — 1
2 Leadership as Love — 13
3 Servant Leadership — 27
4 Transformative Leadership — 39
5 Futuristic Leadership — 53

Bibliography — 63
Index — 67
About the Author — 73

Series Foreword

Historically, the state of Black education has been at the center of American life. When the first Blacks arrived in the Americas to be made slaves, a process of *mis-education* was systematized into the very fabric of American life. Newly arrived Blacks were dehumanized and forced through a process that has been described by a conspicuous slave owner named Willie Lynch as a "breaking process": "Hence the horse and the nigger must be broken; that is, break them from one form of mental life to another—keep the body and take the mind."[1] This horrendous process of breaking Blacks from one form of mental life to another included an elaborate educational system that was designed to kill the creative Black mind.

Elijah Muhammad called this a process that made Black people blind, deaf, and dumb—meaning the minds of Black people were taken from them. He proclaimed, "Back when our fathers were brought here and put into slavery 400 years ago, 300 [of] which they served as servitude slaves, they taught our people everything against themselves."[2] Woodson similarly decried, "Even schools for Negroes, then, are places where they must be convinced of their inferiority. The thought of inferiority of the Negro is drilled into him in almost every class he enters and almost in every book he studies."[3]

Today, Black education seems to be at a crossroads. With the passing of the No Child Left Behind Act of 2001 and Race to the Top, schools that serve a large majority of Black children have been under the scrutiny of politicians who vigilantly proclaim the need to improve schools while not realizing that these schools were never intended to educate or educe the divine powers within Black people.

Watkins posits that after the Civil War, schools for Black people—particularly those in the South—were designed by wealthy philanthropists.[4] These philanthropists designed "seventy-five years of education for blacks."[5] Seventy-five years from 1865 brings us to 1940; one has to consider the historical impact of seventy-five years of scripted education and its influence on the present state of Black education.

Presently, schools are still controlled by an elite ruling class who hold major power. Woodson saw this as a problem in his day and argued, "The education of the Negroes, then, the most important thing in the uplift of Negroes, is almost entirely in the hands of those who have enslaved them and now segregate them."[6] Here, Woodson cogently argues for historical understanding: "To point out merely the defects as they appear today will be of little benefit to the present and future generations. These things must be viewed in their historic setting. The conditions of today have been determined by what has taken place in the past."[7] Watkins summarizes that the "white architects of black education . . . carefully selected and sponsored knowledge, which contributed to obedience, subservience, and political docility."[8] This kind of historical knowledge is essential to understanding the plight of Black education today.

A major historical point in Black education was the famous *Brown v. the Board of Education of Topeka, Kansas*, in which the Supreme Court ruled that segregation deprived Blacks of educational equality. Thus, schools were ordered to integrate with all deliberate speed. This historic ruling has continued to impact the education of Black children in myriad and complex ways.

To date, *Brown v. the Board of Education* has not lived up to the paper that it was printed on. Schools are more segregated today than they were at the time of the *Brown* decision. Even more disheartening is that schools that are supposedly desegregated may have tracking mechanisms such as "gifted and talented" programs that attract White students and give schools the appearance of being integrated while actually creating segregation *within* the school. Spring calls this "second-generation segregation" and asserts: "Unlike segregation that existed by state laws in the South before the 1954 *Brown* decision, second-generation forms of segregation can occur in schools with balanced racial populations; for instance, all White students may be placed in one academic track and all African American or Hispanic students in another track."[9]

In this type of setting, White supremacy may become rooted in the subconscious minds of both Black and White students. Nieto and Bode (2012) highlight the internalized damage that tracking may have on students when they say students "may begin to believe that their placement in these groups is natural and a true reflection of whether they are 'smart,' 'average,' or 'dumb.'"[10]

According to Oakes and Lipton, "African American and Latino students are assigned to low-track classes more often than White (and Asian) students, leading to two separate schools in one building—one [W]hite and one minority."[11] Nieto and Bode argue that the teaching strategy in segregated settings "leaves its mark on pedagogy as well. Students in the lowest levels are most likely to be subjected to rote memorization and static teaching methods."[12] These findings are consistent with Lipman's: "scholars have argued that desegregation policy has been framed by what is in the interest of [W]hites, has abstracted from excellence in education, and has been constructed as racial integration, thus avoiding the central problem of institutional racism."[13] Hammond is not alone, then, in observing that "the school experiences of African American and other minority students in the United States continue to be substantially separate and unequal."[14]

Clearly, the education of Black students must be addressed with a sense of urgency like never before. Lipman alludes to the crisis of Black education, noting that "the overwhelming failure of schools to develop the talents and potentials of students of color is a national crisis."[15] In just about every negative category in education, Black children are overrepresented. Again Lipman explains: "The character and depth of the crisis are only dimly depicted by low achievement scores and high rates of school failure and dropping out."[16]

Under the guise of raising student achievement, the No Child Left Behind Act has instead contributed to the degradation of educational equality for Black students. Hammond cites the negative impact of the law: "The Harvard Civil Rights Project, along with other advocacy groups, has warned that the law threatens to increase the growing dropout rate and pushout rates for students of color, ultimately reducing access to education for these students rather than enhancing it."[17]

Asante summarizes the situation this way: "I cannot honestly say that I have ever found a school in the United States run by whites that adequately prepares black children to enter the world as sane human beings . . . [The school system is] an exploitative, capitalist system that enshrines plantation owners as saints and national heroes cannot possibly create sane black children."[18] The education of Black students and its surrounding issues indeed makes for a national crisis that must be put at the forefront of the African American agenda for liberation.

There is a need for a wide range of scholars, educators, and activists to speak to the issues of educating Black students. In the past, significant scholarly research has been conducted on the education of Black students; however, there does not seem to be a coherent theoretical approach to addressing Black education that is outside of European dominance. Thus, there is a need to examine Black leaders, scholars, activists, and their critique and challenge of power relations in Black education. This idea of challenging power relations is based on the educational philosophies of Elijah Muhammad, Carter G. Woodson, and others whose leadership and ideas could transform schools for Black students.

One can only imagine how schools would look if Elijah Muhammad, Carter G. Woodson, Marcus Garvey, or other significant Black leaders were leading educational institutions. These critical Black educators put the liberation of the mind at the forefront of their philosophies, and this series—Critical Black Pedagogy in Education—is based on the belief that the study of these leaders may serve as the foundation for an entirely new educational system, one that would serve the needs of Black students and in fact all students in the context of our society's diversity. Such a new system would retract the educational agenda from the dominant White powers. As Freire said, "it would be a contradiction in terms if the oppressors not only defended but actually implemented a liberating education."[19]

With Freire's comment in mind, we are looking not only at historical Black leaders but also at the contemporary legacies of these great leaders and the educational leaders who are working today to implement a liberating education. Johnson and colleagues describe the need for this current-day perspective: "There is a need for researchers, educators, policy makers, etc. to comprehend the emancipatory teaching practices that African American teachers employed that in turn contributed to academic success of Black students as well as offered a vision for a more just society."[20]

In service of that goal, the present volume—*Educational Leadership and Louis Farrakhan*—explores the teachings of Louis Farrakhan regarding educational leadership. Many are unaware of the educational aspects of Farrakhan's teachings. Some know of him from his historic Million Man March in Washington, DC, in 1995, a march that drew nearly two million people to the

US Capital, and his leadership of the Nation of Islam. But he has taught extensively about education, and this volume captures his ideas regarding educational philosophy, leadership, critical educational theory, and spirituality.

It is a welcome addition to the literature on Black education. Similar to Joyce King's *Black Education: A Transformative Research and Action Agenda for the New Century*,[21] this book addresses research issues raised in *The Commission on Research in Black Education* (CORIBE). Like CORIBE's agenda, this book focuses on "using culture as an asset in the design of learning environments that are applicable to students' lives and that lead students toward more analytical and critical learning" (p. 353). The book is indeed provocative, compelling, and rich with information that will propel those concerned with equity, justice, and equality of education into a renewed activism.

NOTES

1. K. Hassan-EL, *The Willie Lynch Letter and the Making of Slaves* (Bensenville, IL: Lushena Books, 2007), p. 14.
2. A. Pitre, *The Education Philosophy of Elijah Muhammad: Education for a New World*, 3rd ed. (Lanham, MD: University Press of America, 2015), p. 12.
3. C. G. Woodson, *The Mis-Education of the Negro* (Drewryville, VA: Kha Books, 2008, first edition 1933), p. 2.
4. W. Watkins, *The White Architects of Black Education: Ideology and Power in America 1865–1954* (New York: Teachers College Press, 2001).
5. Watkins, *The White Architects of Black Education*, pp. 41–42.
6. Woodson, *The Mis-Education of the Negro*, p. 22.
7. Woodson, *The Mis-Education of the Negro*, p. 9.
8. Watkins, *The White Architects of Black Education*, p. 40.
9. J. Spring, *American Education* (New York: McGraw Hill, 2006), p. 82.
10. S. Nieto and P. Bode, *Affirming Diversity: The Sociopolitical Context of Multicultural Education*, 6th ed. (Boston: Allyn and Bacon, 2012), p. 111.
11. J. Oakes and M. Lipton, *Teaching to Change the World*, 3rd ed. (Boston: McGraw-Hill, 2007), p. 308.
12. Nieto and Bode, *Affirming Diversity*, p. 111.
13. P. Lipman, *Race and the Restructuring of School* (Albany: SUNY Press, 1998), p. 11.
14. L. Hammond-Darling, "New Standards and Old Inequalities: School Reform and the Education of African American Students," in *Black Education: A Transformative Research and Action Agenda for the New Century*, ed. J. King (Mahwah, NJ: Lawrence Erlbaum Associates, 2005), p. 202.
15. Lipman, *Race and the Restructuring of School*, p. 2.
16. Lipman, *Race and the Restructuring of School*, p. 2.
17. J. Hammond-Darling, "From 'Separate but Equal' to 'No Child Left Behind': The Collision of New Standards and Old Inequalities," in *Many Children Left Behind: How the No*

Child Left Behind Act Is Damaging Our Children and Our Schools, ed. D. Meier and G. Woods (Boston: Beacon Press, 2004), p. 4.

18. M. Asante, *Race, Rhetoric, and Identity: The Architecton of Soul* (Amherst, NY: Humanity Books, 2005), p. 65.

19. P. Freire, *Pedagogy of the Oppressed* (New York: Continuum, 2000), p. 54.

20. K. Johnson, A. Pitre, and K. Johnson, eds., *African American Women Educators: A Critical Examination of Their Pedagogies, Educational Ideas, and Activism from the Nineteenth to the Mid-Twentieth Centuries* (Lanham, MD: Rowman & Littlefield Education, 2014), p. 99.

21. J. King, ed., *Black Education: A Transformative Research and Action Agenda for the New Century* (Mahwah, NJ: Lawrence Erlbaum Associates, 2005).

Preface

Many people became aware of Louis Farrakhan on October 16, 1995, when he brought together nearly two million Black men to Washington, DC, to participate in the Million Man March, dedicated to renewing Black men's leadership in family and community. Prior to the Million Man March, Farrakhan traveled to cities throughout the United States speaking to Black men about awakening to the challenges they faced within a racist society. He addressed the framing of Black men as a menace to society, saying, "[If] you are menace two, who is menace one?"[1]

This tour focused on the challenges Black men faced, and Farrakhan's discussions touched on everything from business and the arts to politics and science. His engagement with academic fields like religious studies, African American studies, political science, and sociology is well known, but very little attention has been given to his contributions to the field of pedagogy and educational leadership.[2] Yet Farrakhan's discourses on education dovetail with the strongest trends in educational theory today, especially concepts found in critical educational theory.

Critical educational scholars are concerned with the inequitable schooling experiences of historically marginalized groups, and their research has covered topics such as social justice, critical race theory, critical pedagogy, and diversity.[3] These are some of the very topics that Farrakhan has discussed throughout years of writing and lecturing on Black education and that the Nation of Islam has addressed through its educational conferences. Through the lens of critical educational theory, Louis Farrakhan offers insights that could transform the schooling experiences of students most marginalized.

The continued emergence of critical educational theory has been most noticeable at major educational conferences such as AERA (American Education Research Association), where the theme for the last few conferences has centered on culture, equity, and social justice.[4] But very few Black educators and theorists are included among the icons of critical educational theory at these conferences. This may be because academics simply don't know of their work or because of the way that Farrakhan and the Nation of Islam have been presented in the mainstream press.

Nonetheless, the teachings of Elijah Muhammad, Louis Farrakhan, and the Nation of Islam have long incorporated ideas that now form the central tenets of what is now known as *critical pedagogy*. There are some exceptions to this neglect. Derrick Bell, for example, one of the pioneers of critical race theory, devoted an entire section of his book *Faces at the Bottom of the Well* to Farrakhan and his ideas.[5]

But critical neglect doesn't mean that Farrakhan's legacy doesn't exist. His influence on critical race theory and education along with other frameworks is evident to those who study his messages with care. Scholars have written about the "savage inequalities" that American schools offer and the plight of urban schools.[6] Farrakhan's educational ideas offer a way out of the terrible conditions that these ethnographies have disclosed. The key to Farrakhan's pedagogy is that Farrakhan, like his teacher Elijah Muhammad, believes that students should be introduced to knowledge that is *transformative*. Paulo Freire might refer to this type of knowledge as *liberatory* because it frees people to discover themselves and their relationship to the larger world.[7]

With this in mind, *Educational Leadership and Louis Farrakhan* introduces for the first time Farrakhan's importance in the field of educational leadership. The reader will find Farrakhan's teachings regarding the purpose of education enlightening. It will challenge educators to rethink their philosophy of education and assist them with articulating a vision for schools and universities that taps human potential. The book explores not only the purpose of education but also concepts such as love, servant leadership, transformative leadership, and futuristic leadership. This seminal book is one step on the journey to discovering why Farrakhan believes that all of these elements are keys to Black liberation.

NOTES

1. L. Farrakhan, "Let Us Make a Man," speech delivered April 11, 1994, Houston, Texas.

2. A. Alexander, *The Farrakhan Factor: African American Writers on Leadership, Nationhood, and Minister Louis Farrakhan* (New York: Grove Press, 1998); L. Fulani and A. Sharpton, *Independent Black Leadership in America: Minister Louis Farrakhan, Dr. Lenora B. Fulani, Reverend Al Sharpton* (New York: Castillo International, 1993); M. Gardell, *In the Name of Elijah Muhammad: Louis Farrakhan and The Nation of Islam* (Durham, NC: Duke University Press, 1996); R. Singh, *The Farrakhan Phenomenon: Race, Reaction, and the Paranoid Style in American Politics* (Washington, DC: Georgetown University Press, 1997); D. Walker, *Islam and the Search for African American Nationhood: Elijah Muhammad, Louis Farrakhan, and the Nation of Islam* (Atlanta: Clarity Press, 2005).

3. M. Apple, *Ideology and Curriculum*, 2nd ed. (New York: Routledge, 2004); J. Banks, *An Introduction to Multicultural Education*, 5th ed. (Boston: Pearson, 2014); C. Marshall and M. Oliva, eds., *Leadership for Social Justice: Making Revolutions in Education*, 2nd ed. (Boston: Pearson, 2009); P. McLaren, *Life in Schools: An Introduction to Critical Pedagogy in the Foundations of Education*, 6th ed. (Boulder, CO: Paradigm, 2015); S. Nieto and P. Bode, *Affirming Diversity: The Sociopolitical Context of Education*, 6th ed. (Boston: Pearson, 2012); A. Pitre, T. Allen, and E. Pitre, eds., *Multicultural Education for Educational Leaders: Critical Race Theory and Antiracist Perspectives* (Lanham, MD: Rowman & Littlefield, 2015); C. Shields, ed., *Transformative Leadership: A Reader* (New York: Peter Lang, 2011); G. Theoharis and M. Scanlan, eds., *Leadership for Increasingly Diverse Schools* (New York: Routledge, 2015).

4. See the American Education Research Association's website (www.aera.net) for a list of annual conference themes.

5. D. Bell, *Faces at the Bottom of the Well: The Permanence of Racism* (New York: Basic Books, 1993).

6. J. Kozol, *Savage Inequalities: Children in America's Schools* (New York: Harper Perennial, 2012).

7. I. Shor and P. Freire, *A Pedagogy for Liberation: Dialogues on Transforming Education* (South Hadley, MA: Bergin & Garvey Publishers, 1987).

Acknowledgments

As with any book, there are several people who have inspired the writing of this book. First, I would like to thank Dr. Dorothy Leflore, former dean of the College of Education at North Carolina A&T State University, for affording me the opportunity to serve as the department chair of Leadership Studies. My experiences at North Carolina A&T State University provided me with answers that I had been seeking. To the faculty and staff at North Carolina A&T State University, I am indeed grateful that our paths crossed (Drs. Ceola Baber, Edward Fort, Comfort Okpala, and Forest Toms). To Ms. Lori Jackson, words cannot express how appreciative I am for your words of inspiration.

In addition to my North Carolina A&T State University family, I would also like to thank my colleagues at Fayetteville State University for the opportunity to serve as department head for Educational Leadership and Foundations. It was during this time that I learned my first lessons of navigating the politics of higher education. Mrs. Mable Hawkins, your wise counsel will forever be cherished!

In my journey from North Carolina to Prairie View A&M University, I have come to realize that PV does indeed produce productive people! I don't think this book would have taken the form that it has if it were not for my experiences at PV. To my PV family, I will forever cherish each of you. To Ms. Edwards, Ms. McFarland, and Ms. Houston, you will never be forgotten for your support. To all of my students, you are my inspiration, and remember that pain brings out creativity.

I am also very appreciative of Sarah Jubar, acquisitions editor at Rowman & Littlefield, for her dedication to the Critical Black Pedagogy in Education series, and to the entire Rowman & Littlefield family for their support. I thank each of you immensely! I am deeply thankful for my copyeditor Lynn Weber for meticulously editing this treasured book. To my close friend Gary; and to my Pastor Dale, thank you for walking with me on this journey of life. Finally, to my immediate family (Ajah, Alaiah, Alijah, Azaiah, and Ruby), thanks for being patient with me.

Introduction

Improving education continues to be an essential platform piece for politicians running for public office in the United States. However, these political leaders are oftentimes the product of the same educational system that they argue is in need of fixing. While nearly everyone agrees that there is a need for a paradigm shift in education, the political leaders making proposals for reform have been shaped by the propaganda of the ruling elite who have governed the educational landscape for decades and indeed centuries. The reforms that they propose may have less to do with education than pushing forward the political aims of those elites. In fact, some scholars contend that the current push for reform is a manufactured crisis created to ultimately lead to the dismantling of public education.[1]

The education of Black people in America has always been a central concern of those shaping the educational landscape. William Watkins, in his book *The White Architects of Black Education,* discloses how the ruling elites have spent considerable amounts of money to ensure that Blacks are schooled to be submissive and docile.[2] Carter G. Woodson likewise recognized this project of educating for conformity rather than knowledge.[3] In his prophetic book *The Mis-Education of the Negro,* he wrote, "The education of the Negroes, then, the most important thing in the uplift of Negroes, is almost entirely in the hands of those who enslaved them and now segregate them."[4] Woodson's declaration is still valid nearly eighty-four years after his writing.

Noam Chomsky has echoed Woodson's work. In his book *Chomsky on Mis-Education,* he asserts that education is designed to control the "bewildered herd"—the masses—to work in the best interest of those ruling the society.⁵ Chomsky notes that the *educated class* or *specialized class* is "a small group of people who analyze, execute, make decisions, and run things in the political, economic, and ideological systems."⁶

One important way in which the ruling elites have continued to impose this domesticating agenda is through education-preparation programs. In colleges that prepare teachers for public education, student teachers are taught that education is a matter of conveying technical knowledge. They are not exposed to the idea that education can serve the purpose of domesticating or liberating.

Domesticating education confines and restricts people's ability to be free. In fact, education fits them into a human capitalist ideology that needs their labor for the production of wealth. To that end, the system of education continues to keep the wealthy in dominant positions because it gives them more capital to expend, thus creating monopolies that allow them to ultimately shape the people's thinking without them ever knowing the origin of their thoughts. McLaren identifies this practice as hegemony: "The dominant class need not impose force for the manufacture of hegemony, since the subordinate class actively subscribes to many of the values and objectives of the dominant class without being aware of the source of those values or the interest that informs them."⁷

Popular culture plays a part in the dissemination of the dominant ideology. Television and radio project a vision of life into the psyche of the masses that has its origins in the dominant mindset. One function of ideology in popular culture is to create an image of Blacks as bestial and dangerous. As a result of these images, whether in school or at the mall or in their neighborhoods, Black youth become targets of their peers, law enforcement, and others.

Education works in collaboration with this cultural project. It fails to create a consciousness in Black youth that they are being socially engineered to behave in ways that "justify" violence and even homicide against them. It fails to communicate the inequitable conditions that exist in society. Instead, they are schooled to support the dominant class, and having completed school, they are paid minimum wage for their labor.⁸

Elijah Muhammad observed this dynamic early on. He saw that the purpose of education in the United States was largely to produce workers who would deliver profits to the ruling elite: "Why should we spend 12 and 16 years seeking an education only to give the benefit of our knowledge back to the one we sought it from? It is time for us to wake up! Why should we give the meager earnings of our labor back to our slave-masters' children?"[9]

Bowles and Gintis, in their book *Schooling in Capitalist America,* describe education through the lens of social reproduction theory. Social reproduction theory contends that schools reproduce the inequities that exist in the society.[10] Prior to the term *social reproduction,* Malcolm X articulated the same premise based on education inequality: "When you live in a poor neighborhood, you . . . have poor schools, when you have poor schools, you have poor teachers, when you have poor teachers, you get a poor education, poor education, you can only work on a poor-paying job, and that poor-paying job enables you to live again in a poor neighborhood; so it is a very vicious cycle."[11]

Many theorists have come to the same conclusion since Malcolm X first spoke about it. Peter McLaren, a leading critical educational theorist, writes that the labor of oppressed groups is at the core of many of the inequalities that exist in society. In his book *Pedagogy of Insurrection*, he writes, "The chief executive officer of our Walmart stores, Michael Duke, makes US $16,826.92 an hour whereas new employees making $8.75 an hour gross $13,650 a year."[12] Chomsky writes, "Far from creating independent thinkers, schools have always, throughout history, played an institutional role in system of control and coercion. And once you are educated, you have already been socialized in ways to support the power structure, which, in turn rewards you immensely."[13]

Joel Spring asserts that a human capitalist ideology—which sees students merely as future workers—is driving educational policy in the twenty-first century.[14] Students educated to become docile workers are blind to the inequities that form the basis of the ruling elite's hegemony. McLaren writes, "Hegemony is a struggle in which the powerful win the consent of those who are oppressed, with the oppressed unknowingly participating in their own oppression."[15]

These hegemonic interests are clearly at work in the push for educational reform today. Under the cloak of slogans like "No Child Left Behind" or "Race to the Top," they are proposing initiatives to further monitor and control what students learn and how they think. Macedo acknowledges this objective when he says of educators, "As paid functionaries of the state, teachers are expected to engage in a form of moral, social, political, and economic reproduction designed to shape students in the image of the dominant society."[16]

Today school boards and legislative bodies are filled with persons who have been schooled to maintain the existing inequalities. The masses are unconscious of the "shadow government" that works in the best interest of a small few while leaving the masses to never discover their divine essence. Spring, in his book *The Politics of American Education,* discusses the "shadow education system" that dictates policy in the elites' best interest: "Consequently, the shadow education system and multinational testing corporations are interested in public acceptance of human capital ideology and the legitimization of assessment-driven school systems."[17]

These challenges raise questions around leadership. Too often, those in leadership roles are working in the best interest of the powerful. At worst, they are doing so consciously. At best, they are operating in ignorance regarding the hidden forces that are shaping policies that negatively impact those who do not belong to the dominant class. There is a leadership crisis, and when effective leadership emerges, there is a wave of propaganda used to silence authentic leaders.

Louis Farrakhan, leader of the Nation of Islam, has for decades written about these very issues that form the core of educational theory today.[18] He has not only critiqued dominant educational practice but has also actively created schools across the country to educate the oppressed and historically underserved. And yet his contribution to the field of education has been overshadowed by the dominant culture's demonization of him in the public square. He, like so many other Black educators, has been excluded from professional recognition.

Ricky Allen notes that Blacks are absent in conferences on critical pedagogy despite their activism of working in the best interest of the oppressed. He writes, "How can the critical pedagogy community claim to be on the side of the oppressed when the members of the two most historically oppressed groups in United States (and throughout the Americas), Blacks and Indians, don't show up to our events or have a strong, leading presence in critical pedagogy scholarship (bell hooks, aside)."[19]

It is clear that prior to the Frankfurt School of thought, there was a cadre of critical Africana theorists who offered a critique of society and education that continue to speak to us in the twenty-first century.[20] Michael Apple writes that before the term *critical* was applied, there were Blacks who were doing critical educational scholarship.[21] A careful reading of the historical literature posits that critical Black pedagogues offered a critique of education and society that predated the European founders of critical educational theory. Furthermore these critical Black educators offered a critique of education that was matchless.

For critical educational theorists and their students, Farrakhan is problematic because his critiques also offer solutions to the crisis of education, which takes power out of the White space and places it squarely at the control of those who have been oppressed. Farrakhan offers a powerful critique of education, and his articulation of knowledge goes beyond the wall of the academic canon of knowledge, freeing him from concepts that have enslaved those who have been educated to stay in their place. And because Farrakhan is not seeking tenure and promotion or an educational leadership position controlled by those who rule the society he is able to educate or awaken the divine essence in human beings. Paulo Freire called this type of education one that makes people conscious.[22] Farrakhan is continuing along a continuum of great prophets and teachers who disrupted the status quo to free human beings from those bestriding the land and using their power to trample on the least of these.

This volume introduces the educational ideas of Louis Farrakhan alongside several leading scholars in education. It offers to educators a contribution that if carefully studied will open up a new way of viewing society and education. The book contains five chapters that specifically speak to education and educational leadership.

Chapter 1 explores the purpose of education drawing from Minister Farrakhan's books *A Torchlight for America* and *Education Is the Key*.[23] The chapter is designed to help educators reflect on the purpose of education, causing them to question how they have developed their philosophical views toward education. One of the major goals listed in the preparation standards of educational leaders is competency in developing a shared vision. Vision is based on one's knowledge, which is grounded in philosophy. So for educational leaders, one has to reflect on the purpose of education.

Chapter 2, "Leadership as Love," explores a lecture by Minister Farrakhan titled "Principles and Practices of Leadership to Suffice Our Needs," where he offers powerful explanations of leadership. The chapter begins by defining leadership using Peter G. Northouse's definition of leadership along with others; it is explored in the context of leadership principles needed to effectively guide educational leadership practice.[24] Principles such as *forgiveness, empowerment, humility, listening, selflessness, perseverance,* and *intelligence* are explored in this chapter.

Chapter 3 explores servant leadership, a concept coined by Robert Greenleaf, which Minister Farrakhan sees as the cornerstone of leadership.[25] During Farrakhan's sixty-plus years of leadership, he has personified servant leadership, earning him the name "The Minister" which means servant. Not only has he practiced servant leadership, but he has also taught about the principles of servant leadership. This chapter extracts from Abraham Maslow's hierarchy of needs, highlighting that servant leaders attend to the needs of the people in the organization.

In chapter 4, transformative leadership is discussed comparatively to Farrakhan's teaching on education and leadership. It discusses critical educational theory to disclose how those in power have shaped an educational agenda to keep the masses from being conscious. It reviews Carolyn Shield's (2011) work on transformative leadership offering an enriched discussion that can help educational leaders to navigate the turbulent political agendas that are negatively impacting the education of historically underserved groups.[26]

In the concluding chapter, "Futuristic Leadership," Farrakhan's ideas about education and educational leadership are discussed in the context of current challenges facing educational leaders. It explores the necessity of a paradigm shift in our thinking about these educational challenges. It highlights the need to think about future educational leaders who will be needed in a new and better world. The chapter draws from the work of Margaret Wheatley's book *Finding Our Way: Leadership for Uncertain Times*.[27] Using concepts in organizational development and change, it relates these concepts to Minister Farrakhan's article "Truth: The Principle of Organization."[28]

NOTES

1. David Berliner and Bruce Biddle, *The Manufactured Crisis: Myths, Fraud and the Attack on America's Public Schools* (New York: Addison Wesley, 1995); Gerald Bracey, *What You Should Know about the War against America's Public Schools* (New York: Allyn and Bacon, 2002).

2. William Watkins, *The White Architects of Black Education: Ideology and Power in America 1865–1954* (New York: Teachers College Press, 2001).

3. Carter G. Woodson, *The Mis-Education of the Negro* (Chicago: African American Images, 1933).

4. Woodson, *The Mis-Education of the Negro*, p. 22.

5. Noam Chomsky, *Chomsky on Mis-Education* (Lanham, MD: Rowman & Littlefield, 2000).

6. Chomsky, *Chomksy on Mis-Education*, p. 22.

7. Chomsky, *Chomksy on Mis-Education*, p. 141.
8. Chomsky, *Chomksy on Mis-Education*.
9. Elijah Muhammad, *Message to the Blackman in America* (Chicago: Final Call, 1965), p. 57.
10. Samuel Bowles and Herbert Gintis, *Schooling in Capitalist America: Educational Reform and the Contradictions of Economic Life* (Chicago: Haymarket Books, 2011).
11. Retrieved from: https://www.youtube.com/watch?v=eVcw9IValHE, on June 29, 2016.
12. Peter McLaren, *Pedagogy of Insurrections: From Resurrection to Revolution* (New York: Peter Lang, 2015), p. 68.
13. Chomsky, *Chomksy on Mis-Education*, p. 3.
14. McLaren, *Pedagogy of Insurrections*.
15. McLaren, *Pedagogy of Insurrections*, p. 140.
16. Cited in Chomsky, *Chomksy on Mis-Education*, p. 3.
17. Joel Spring, *The Politics of American Education* (New York: Routledge, 2011), p. 5.
18. Louis Farrakhan, *A Torchlight for America* (Chicago: Final Call, 1993); Louis Farrakhan, *Education Is the Key* (Chicago: Final Call, 2006).
19. Rickey Allen, "The Race Problem in Critical Pedagogy Community," in *Reinventing Critical Pedagogy: Widening The Circle of Anti-Oppression Education*, ed. Ricky Allen and Marc Pruyn, pp. 3–21 (Lanham, MD: Rowman & Littlefield, 2006), p. 4.
20. Reiland Rabaka, *Du Bois's Dialectics: Black Radical Politics and the Reconstruction of Critical Social Theory* (Lanham, MD: Lexington Books, 2008).
21. Michael Apple, Wayne Au, and Luis Gandin, eds., *The Routledge International Handbook of Critical Education* (New York: Routledge, 2009).
22. Paulo Freire, *Pedagogy of the Oppressed* (New York: Continuum, 2000).
23. Farrakhan, *A Torchlight for America*; Farrakhan, *Education Is the Key*.
24. Peter Northouse, *Leadership: Theory and Practice* (Thousand Oaks, CA: Sage, 2016).
25. Robert Greenleaf, *Servant Leadership: A Journey into the Nature of Legitimate Power and Greatness* (Mahwah, NJ: Paulist Press, 2002).
26. Carolyn Shields, ed., *Transformative Leadership: A Reader* (New York: Peter Lang, 2011).
27. Margaret Wheatley, *Finding Our Way: Leadership for Uncertain Times* (San Francisco Berrett-Koehler, 2007).
28. L. Farrakhan, "Truth, the Principle of Organization." Retrieved from http://www.finalcall.com/columns/mlf/mlf-organization.html, on June 29, 2016.

Chapter One

The Purpose of Education

Educators very seldom have the opportunity to reflect on the purpose of education. Most educator preparation programs require courses on the philosophy of education. However, these courses are primarily academic and rote—not a starting point to think about one's personal practice of education. Most important, these classes do not provide students with an understanding of the significant role that the education profession plays in shaping society.

Louis Farrakhan has written and spoken extensively on the purpose of education. This chapter explores the purpose of education in the context of Farrakhan's educational ideas.

THE DOMINANT MODEL

Truly thinking about the function of education is an innovative enterprise. The basics of education—reading, writing, and arithmetic—seem obvious to most people. But education in the United States has always been guided by specific interests for specific purposes. Educational theorists like Noam Chomsky, Peter McLaren, and Joel Spring have detailed how business elites have developed and implemented educational policies specifically to meet their needs for workers.[1] For Black students, these policies have been developed by Whites in order to train Blacks for their subservient role in the society.[2] This type of "education for domestication" has been the premise of modern schooling.

The central premise of this domestication is that education is intended to deposit information and certain skills into the students rather than to develop students in all of their capabilities and humanity. The latest strategy for this is a common-core curriculum and high-stakes testing. Students have become data and teachers have become deskilled technocrats who implement a curriculum and instructional models designed to reproduce the required data in students' minds.

Paulo Freire, in his seminal book, *Pedagogy of the Oppressed*, developed a metaphor of education as banking, in which teachers deposit information into students.[3] The students in the banking model of education are storage devices; they do not have a realness that is found in living things. The constant pressure to consume information and then regurgitate it on demand causes students to lose their thirst for knowledge. The steadily increasing dislike of knowledge ensures that students will turn away from the pursuit of ideas—ideas that might free their hearts and minds to change the world and fully realize their potential. Even those students who embrace and enjoy education end up working within the sphere of those in the dominant positions; thus their talent becomes a resource for the ruling elite rather than a conduit for liberation or change.

The banking model—which ultimately discourages interest in ideas—is not the only problem with the current reality of education. The dominant elites determine not only *how* information is to be deposited (rather than, for example, talents are to be developed) but also *what* information is deposited. Critical educational scholars like Michael Apple have addressed this issue head-on. Apple, in his book *Ideology and Curriculum*, raises the following questions: "Whose knowledge is it? Who selected it? Why is it organized and taught in this way? To this particular group?"[4] Much earlier, in the 1930s, Carter G. Woodson admonished, "The mere imparting of information is not education. Above all things, the effort must result in making a man think and do for himself."[5]

Louis Farrakhan has offered his own critique of the control of information that is fed to students: "White people allowed Black people to come to school, and learn to read and write, but they wrote the books that Black people read so that they would be sure to know what Black people would write."[6] Even the movement toward multicultural education has not really addressed the underlying issues. Schools may now occasionally highlight Black contributions to the world, but James Banks has noted the insufficiency of these measures. Banks says that the contributions approach consists of adding "heroes, holidays and discrete cultural elements" without changing the structure of the curriculum. Even what Banks calls the additive approach—adding entire units on non-dominant cultures—still leaves the dominant perspective intact.[7]

At its worst, these types of multicultural efforts can actually be counterproductive. Many multicultural education scholars have noted that adding token persons from diverse groups does not truly align with the goals of multicultural education. Nieto and Bode provide an example of tokenism in the schools' treatment of Martin Luther King Jr. They argue that King has been converted from the criticalist that he was into a milquetoast by those who have engineered the history books.[8]

FARRAKHAN'S CRITIQUE OF THE DOMINANT MODEL

As early as the 1960s, Louis Farrakhan began to develop a powerful critique of the dominant White model of education for Black students. He had a mentor in Elijah Muhammad, who himself responded to the education question: "We have been to schools where they do not teach us the knowledge of self. We have been to the schools of our slave-master's children. We have been to their schools and gone as far as they allowed us to go."[9] In his 1965 volume *Message to the Blackman in America,* Muhammad emphasized the need for Blacks to take control of their own education.

Farrakhan, following the same line of reasoning, writes: "We don't have to ask why we should control our education. The answer is clear. We should control it because if we don't we will always be under somebody else's control."[10] Farrakhan, expanding on this train of thought in a 1992 lecture at the Muhammad University of Islam, noted: "He who gives you the diameter of your knowledge prescribes the circumference of your activities. If your slave-master is your educator, no wonder you act like a slave."[11]

These statements reflected the questions that other scholars in the area of curriculum have raised about the education process. Deciding on what body of knowledge should be included in the curriculum is a political question. For those in positions of power, the questions of what knowledge and whose knowledge are of utmost importance because it is this knowledge incorporated into the curriculum that can ultimately dictate one's action. Woodson was insightful when he wrote, "When you control a man's thinking you do not have to worry about his actions. . . . You do not have to tell him to stand here or go yonder. He will find his proper place and will stay in it."[12]

For the Nation of Islam, the education question went hand in hand with the question of economic dependency. Elijah Muhammad argued, "Our former slave-masters, knowing our dependence upon them, maliciously and hatefully adopted attitudes and social and educational systems that have deprived us of the opportunity to become free and independent right up to the present day."[13] To use education to become independent economically is the foundation for true freedom.

Accordingly, the Nation of Islam under the leadership of Elijah Muhammad stressed that Blacks in America needed to set up their own banking system where they could deposit millions of dollars from the pooled money into an economic savings plan: "These quarters will be banked until we have a million dollars to begin building a banking system."[14] The economics savings plan would also produce money to buy land, which is the basis for freedom because it is from the land that you receive all the essentials necessary to survive.

Just as the education issue flowed into economic independence, economics and culture were also entwined. Elijah Muhammad wrote, "We like sport and play, but we suffer the pains of hunger because of the millions of dollars lost paying notes for luxuries we could do without—such as fine automobiles, fine clothes, whiskey, beer, wine, cigarettes, tobacco and drugs."[15] Elijah Muhammad is not saying that Blacks should not attain material luxuries, however; he is arguing that as a collective group, if Blacks pooled their resources before individually seeking these luxuries, in the long term they would be able to own a world. Today drugs, alcohol, and other vices are marketed directly to youth in efforts to engineer and control thought.

Farrakhan continued to develop this line of thought, exposing those who are making tremendous wealth from Black entertainment while negatively shaping worldviews toward them. In a speech at Tennessee State University titled "Business Is Warfare," he raised the question around ownership of professional basketball teams, a key example of Blacks producing the wealth that is appropriated by non-Black owners and elites.[16] Taking the reins of Black economic life through education has been key for the Nation of Islam. Elijah Muhammad succinctly wrote, "How long shall we seek the white men's education to become their servants instead of becoming builders of a progressive nation of our own on some of this earth we can call our own?"[17]

With regard to those controlling the educational system, Farrakhan argues that the current educational model ultimately supports White supremacy: "If a people are going to rule, they have to have an ideology and philosophy that undergirds and guides the education so that the people who are going to rule can rule."[18]

The dominant education now is designed to keep that rule firmly within White control: "We were mis-educated and taught against ourselves, so our education was not real because it was not based on completed truth. It was based on the psychology of White supremacy and reinforced in the minds of Black people that we must accept our subhuman posture and position and remember that White people are born to rule and we must never rise to challenge that rule."[19]

Educational scholars in the areas of multicultural education, critical race studies, and critical White studies have acknowledged the White supremacist ideology that undergirds educational practice. So how can we develop an alternative that provides true education and eliminates the ideology of Black inferiority and domestication?

FARRAKHAN'S NEW MODEL OF EDUCATION

Scholars in multicultural education like James Banks have ventured to explore the curriculum and, moreover, have written that multicultural education at its core is about freedom, justice, and equality.[20] These are the very principles that Louis Farrakhan has espoused in terms of Black liberation. Farrakhan does not prescribe to the current idea that education should be solely focused on getting a job. For Farrakhan, education has a much bigger purpose, which is to bring human beings into oneness with the Creator.[21] To him, education is a key that can either unlock human potential or keep human potential locked up.

Education for Farrakhan involves awakening the creative mind in people: "Education must lead out or cultivate what God has put within so that the world can glorify God by seeing what God has deposited in each human."[22] Farrakhan articulates that education is rooted in the Latin prefix "e" and "duco." The "duco" means "to lead," and the prefix "e" means "out from." Education leads people out of the darkness into the light, bringing forth ideas and creative thought from within them.

The concept of education for the purpose of stimulating ideas has been discussed by philosophers for centuries. Socrates believed that ideas were already present in the human being but needed to be brought to the forefront of one's consciousness. Similarly, the Nation of Islam believes that education should illuminate the ability of students to do something for themselves, to elicit their inner potential to change their lives and their world.

This process of unveiling students' potential through education is not only intellectual but also deeply spiritual. Knowledge of their true selves liberates students in a way that the banking model of education can never do. Farrakhan used the life of Malcolm X as an example in this regard: In Malcolm we see "a young man who looks like many young men today, except that he rose from a low-life of crime and ignorance, into the man who a great many now admire. Malcolm rose to heights because he was taught the knowledge of God, self and others by The Honorable Elijah Muhammad"[23]

The knowledge of self has in fact been the basis for ruling-class education in Europe for thousands of years. Knowledge of self cultivates the divinity that is in all human beings and unlocks their freedom and potentiality. As John Taylor Gatto writes, "at the core of this elite system of education is the belief that self-knowledge is the only basis for true knowledge."[24] Education that includes the knowledge of self frees the individual, so they can no longer be held captive to those who rule.

Educational thinkers like Farrakhan have proposed a broader idea of multicultural education. At the higher end of the multicultural spectrum would be an understanding of perspectives that each person might have toward a particular concept. An even higher level of education would be encouraging students to make decisions and take action to resolve social issues. Like critical educational scholars, Farrakhan encourages a serious examination of what is being taught to students that might cause them to internalize negative self-images that are based on race, ethnicity, culture, or gender.

In the area of critical White studies, scholars in education have sought ways to undo White supremacy. They have argued that Whiteness is a type of property that gives Whites added value. This added value in conjunction with White supremacist ideology should be explored from its origin.

Farrakhan in 1993 offered a potent critique not only of White supremacy but also of education's role in perpetuating or combating it: "One of the things that separates man from beast is knowledge. Knowledge feeds the development of the human being so that the person can grow and evolve into Divine and become one with The Creator. It's not one's maleness or femaleness, being Black or being White, rather it is our growth and reflection of knowledge that distinguishes us from the lower forms of life."[25]

Clearly, knowledge is the key, but what knowledge is of most value? Farrakhan believes the knowledge of God and self should be the basis for curriculum development. In speaking about the success of students attending the Muhammad University of Islam, he points out that the students are taught that each of the subjects they study is part of the self. Mastery of the subjects is truly mastery of yourself. He writes, "A new public school system should relate the curriculum to the self. When we see the curriculum as an outgrowth of self, then we can identify with the curriculum giving us an incentive to learn. In the Muhammad University of Islam school system, our students' learning is facilitated because they identify with the subjects. They are taught they are the subject. They are taught, I am chemistry."[26]

For Farrakhan, it is important for students to be taught the knowledge of self because this will allow students to develop a respect for self and others. It also stimulates in students the thirst for knowledge. Elijah Muhammad in 1965 wrote, "Knowledge of self makes you take on the great virtue of learning."[27] It is the knowledge of self that awakens the student to the teacher within. Once the teacher within is tapped, the student is on a lifelong journey in the search for knowledge that will satisfy their appetite. Knowledge is likened unto spiritual food in the sense that it nourishes the spiritual development of the human being, causing them to see and live on the highest plane of existence.

Farrakhan spoke about the "teacher within." He pointed out that a baby learns more in the first year of life than in all of their years of living combined.[28] How does this happen, he asks, without a teacher with a lesson plan? It is because there is a teacher within. And like the teacher within, there is a knowledge that goes beyond books that students are not allowed to truly study. He writes, "When we came forth from the wombs of our mothers we were birthed into a Book, a pure Book; a Book that is all Truth. We have the heavens above and the earth beneath, and everything around us is truth and everything around is a book."[29]

Then he goes on to discuss how, when Blacks were slaves, they learned to read the universe: "How do you know that trouble won't last always Grandma? *Because the snow and the ice don't last always child.* Grandma I hear the slave-master in church singing and talking about Jesus rising from the dead. What do you think about that? *Child, yes, the seed seems to sleep or die in winter, but it rises again in the spring. So do not worry because you appear to be sleeping now, child. Just hold on, your rise is coming.*"[30]

THE ROLE OF TEACHERS IN SPIRITUAL EDUCATION

The knowledge of self does not only include the student; it must first begin with the teacher. For Farrakhan, the teacher is the key in the learning process.

Teachers in today's society have been reduced to technicians, and they are not being educated to see the profession as a prophetic calling. The spiritual teachers of the discipline recognize the deep meaning and purpose for studying a particular discipline and have the ability to make the discipline come alive for students. In fact, spiritual teachers have the ability to awaken in students a curiousness that will cause them to gravitate to a particular area of study.

Spiritual teachers take more time to develop than the normal classroom teacher, and this is precisely what Elijah Muhammad did as a teacher. He developed a thirst for knowledge of the universe, meaning knowledge that is all encompassing. This is echoed in Farrakhan's writings when he declares, "So if you are cognizant of the law upon which this universe is constructed—and it is a just law and just balance—then you are careful about what you do to others, because you do not want it done to you."[31]

In the area of education, one of the major concepts that educators should be cognizant of is teacher expectations. Teacher expectations have an impact on student disposition toward learning. In a study by Rosenthal and Jacobson, teachers were given faulty data that indicated that their students were prodigies when in fact they were no smarter than other students in the class.[32] Based on this information, the researchers observed that the teachers created a supportive climate for students, provided more feedback, and gave these students more response time. At the end of the school year, these students experienced significant increases in their IQ scores. The Pygmalion effect, as it came to be labeled, introduced the concept that teacher expectations play a major role in the education process.

In part, the Nation of Islam's expectation for teaching and learning was specifically designed to awaken what they describe as the "God consciousness." Malcolm X with his criminal record would never have been admitted into the lowest rung colleges or universities. Elitist institutions would have denied him admission, claiming that he could not successfully matriculate through college. But what Elijah Muhammad saw in these young people he mentored was a God within that needed cultivation, and it was through the knowledge of self that he created intellectual giants.

While the cultural deprivation theory looks at the student's home environment as a failure, Farrakhan cherishes the opportunity to teach those on the margins of society. Dr. Abdulalim Shabazz, one of the great math teachers and a student of Elijah Muhammad who encouraged Black students to pursue advanced degrees in mathematics, said, "Give me your worst ones and I will teach them."[33] Speaking to his success with students, he pointed out that "his approach was to *appeal to the intellect* of each and every student, *to their humanity*, and *their reasoning.*"[34] Embedded in this statement are teacher expectations—powerful expectations of achievement that help explain Shabazz's great success in mentoring his students.

At the core of the education process in the Nation of Islam is the belief that "you are all Gods." This in turn creates a different learning environment, one that brings out creative ideas. The teaching model according to Farrakhan should be Jesus. McLaren discusses the teachings of Jesus to shatter many of the myths that underlie the current educational practice that is rooted in human capitalist ideology. In his chapter titled "Comrade Jesus," McLaren writes: "Clearly the message of Jesus is to create the Kingdom of God on earth, as it has been created in heaven. Jesus is the prototypical rebel, someone whom suburban U.S. parents would continuously warn their children to avoid, and certainly not befriend."[35]

Farrakhan preceded McLaren in introducing Jesus as the key education figure.[36] For Farrakhan, Jesus represents education itself. He points out that the world is awaiting a man with tremendous knowledge, a messiah, and "the Messiah is Education." Unlike those who see human beings as future workers, Farrakhan contends, "The Messiah is a person full of knowledge that the world has deprived the people of; a person coming that is the way, the truth, and the light. He is a person coming that will show you the right method that is the key to unlock doors that have been locked against you."[37] This Messiah educator challenges and disrupts that status quo of the society by sharing knowledge that builds character. He offers "a method, a way, a truth and a life that is above savage existence that you have right now, with your false degrees and lack of character."[38]

Farrakhan takes issue with the marketing of degrees by colleges and universities that fail to provide sufficient knowledge to transform or grow human beings. Just as the sports and entertainment industries rob Blacks of their money, so does the education industry rob them of the opportunity to develop their true selves. They have been locked away from discovering the beauty that exists within them in order to maintain their worker function in society.

CONCLUSION

Farrakhan points out that we come out of the earth, and like the earth, one has to dig into the earth to discover its treasures. Thus education has a leading-out force that helps one to uncover the treasures and power of their being. Like critical theorists in education, he challenges those who have used education and schooling as a tool to wax rich while the masses suffer, causing him to say, "Take knowledge and let it give you a heart for the suffering people who are your own and the suffering people of the world. Take knowledge and let it strengthen your will to see men free, justified, and equal."[39]

Educational scholars concerned with issues of equity and justice appear to recognize that a battle is being fought to liberate human beings. These battles are usually described in political language but have a spiritual language that is neglected. Speaking to this, Farrakhan writes, "The powers of this world do not want a better life for the masses of people, whether they are White or Black. The powers of this world are here to lock people out of the Kingdom of God, by depriving them of knowledge that will let them go free from this world and open up a new world."[40] A better life is one that produces love, because human beings will begin to see the beautiful qualities existing within themselves, thus giving meaning and purpose to their lives. Education and love are synonymous and will be explored more deeply in the succeeding chapters.

NOTES

1. Noam Chomsky, *Chomsky on Mis-Education* (Lanham, MD: Rowman & Littlefield, 2000); Peter McLaren, *Pedagogy of Insurrections: From Resurrection to Revolution* (New York: Peter Lang, 2015); Joel Spring, *The Politics of American Education* (New York: Routledge, 2011).

2. William Watkins, *The White Architects of Black Education: Ideology and Power in America 1865–1954* (New York: Teachers College Press, 2001); Donald Spivey, *Schooling for the New Slavery: Black Industrial Education, 1868–1915* (Trenton, NJ: Africa World Press, 2007).

3. Paulo Freire, *Pedagogy of the Oppressed* (New York: Continuum, 2000).

4. Michael Apple, *Ideology and Curriculum* (New York: Routledge, 2004), p. 6.

5. Carter G. Woodson, *The Mis-Education of the Negro* (Chicago: African American Images, 1933), p. 20.

6. Louis Farrakhan, *Education Is the Key* (Chicago: Final Call, 2006), p. 20.

7. J. A. Banks, *An Introduction to Multicultural Education* (Upper Saddle River, NJ: Pearson, 2014), p. 54.

8. S. Nieto and P. Bode, *Affirming Diversity: The Sociopolitical Context of Education* (Upper Saddle River, NJ: Pearson, 2014).

9. Elijah Muhammad, *Message to the Blackman in America* (Chicago: Final Call, 1965), p. 34.
10. Muhammad, *Message to the Blackman in America*.
11. Louis Farrakhan, "Why We Must Control the Education of Our Children," speech delivered at the Second Annual Muhammad University of Islam Banquet, August 15, 1992, Chicago, http://www.finalcall.com/columns/mlf-education.html.
12. Woodson, *The Mis-Education of the Negro*, p. 21.
13. Muhammad, *Message to the Blackman in America*, p. 227.
14. Muhammad, *Message to the Blackman in America*, p. 193.
15. Muhammad, *Message to the Blackman in America*, p. 193.
16. Retrieved from: https://www.youtube.com/watch?v=vKUYRDmxmWk on July 1, 2016.
17. Muhammad, *Message to the Blackman in America*, p. 221.
18. Farrakhan, "Why We Must Control the Education of Our Children."
19. Farrakhan, *Education Is the Key*, p. 21.
20. Banks, *An Introduction to Multicultural Education*.
21. Farrakhan, *Education Is the Key*.
22. Farrakhan, "Why We Must Control the Education of Our Children."
23. Louis Farrakhan, *A Torchlight for America* (Chicago: Final Call, 1993), p. 49.
24. John Taylor Gatto, *Dumbing Us Down: The Hidden Curriculum of Compulsory Schooling* (Gabriola Island, BC: New Society Publishers, 2005), p. 30.
25. Farrakhan, *Torchlight for America*, p. 47.
26. Farrakhan, *Torchlight for America*, p. 49.
27. Muhammad, *Message to the Blackman in America*, p. 39.
28. Farrakhan, *Education Is the Key*.
29. Farrakhan, *Education Is the Key*, p. 16.
30. Farrakhan, *Education Is the Key*, p. 17.
31. Farrakhan, *Education Is the Key*, p. 17.
32. Robert Rosenthal and Lenore Jacobson, *Pygmalion in the Classroom: Teacher Expectations and Pupils' Intellectual Development* (Wales, UK: Crown House Publishing, 1992).
33. A. Hilliard, *The Marron within Us: Selected Essays on African American Socialization. Baltimore* (Baltimore: Black Classic Press, 1995), p. 195.
34. Hilliard, *The Marron within Us*, p. 196.
35. Peter McLaren, *Pedagogy of Insurrection: From Resurrection to Revolution* (New York: Peter Lang. 2015), p. 105.
36. Farrakhan, *Education Is the Key*.
37. Farrakhan, *Education Is the Key*, p. 26.
38. Farrakhan, *Education Is the Key*, p. 27.
39. Farrakhan, *Education Is the Key*, p. 29.
40. Farrakhan, *Education Is the Key*, p. 28.

Chapter Two

Leadership as Love

Leadership is the catalyst that moves people toward a common goal. Northouse writes regarding leadership that "leadership is a process whereby an individual influences a group of individuals to achieve a common goal."[1] John Maxwell, a leadership expert, puts it even more succinctly: "Leadership is influence. That's it. Nothing more; nothing less."[2]

Educational leaders today are faced with an enormous amount of change within the educational landscape. They find themselves resolving conflicts, attending meetings, ensuring paperwork is processed, and being responsible for the overall operation of the institution they lead. They are faced with the ongoing political debates about educational policy. The violence that has permeated schools and universities, the student and teacher apathy, and the need to improve test scores on a yearly basis make the job of educational leaders extremely difficult.

To address these challenges, several educational-leadership preparation programs are revising their curricula to better prepare teachers and administrators for their new and complex roles. Education is in need of leaders who can move educational institutions beyond the technocracy that is centered on test scores, data banks, and assessment models that educational leaders are tasked with managing.

While the majority of preparation programs for educational leaders are centered on the technical aspects of the position, including social justice principles of leadership in educational-leadership preparation programs could transform education in important ways. In the twenty-first century, several educational-leadership programs are beginning to focus on leadership rather than management, and in doing so, they have begun to explore concepts such as leadership for diversity and social justice.

MANAGEMENT (VERSUS LEADERSHIP)

Leadership is not the same as management. Managers are charged with maintaining the day-to-day operations of schools within the rules set forth by the school or university systems where they work. Often they are so overloaded with this task that they seldom have opportunities to interact with the people in the organization in any sustained, meaningful way.

In some schools and universities, this lack of communication and teamwork leads to an us-versus-them mentality in which administrators see themselves as separate from the masses of people with whom they work, and vice versa. Peter Block writes, "There is the dominant belief that leadership should come from the top and bosses are in some way responsible for their employees performance and morale. . . . We have created a class system inside our institutions. There is a management class and an employee class."[3]

This type of division is harmful to the organization, and administrators can often be found speaking negatively about the people they are charged with leading. In their minds, leaders must carry a big stick and use it in order to keep faculty and staff in line. One longtime administrator put it this way: "The leader must have an iron hand. They must be ready to crush the people in the organization if they do not follow the manager's orders."

John Hoyle writes, "These boss codes of behavior make it easier to reprimand, control, or lay off employees."[4] Even in the organization of the buildings where people work, administrators are most often isolated. Their offices are usually on the highest floor. And while managers do need space to think and envision changes, this isolation can make them lose touch with their staff and the reality of their schools.

This disjunction can make educational centers chaotic and reflect what is derogatively referred to as *street life*. *Street life* is used to describe some schools and universities that are unfocused and unmoored, where faculty, staff, and students are just trying to survive. It refers to schools and districts where administrators and teachers are locked in a hostile relationship. Street life prevails when administrators are chosen for their management focus, for their skill at carrying out the priorities of the elites that direct educational policy: cost-cutting, control, and regulation.

LEADERSHIP (VERSUS MANAGEMENT)

If management is concerned with day-to-day operations, cost-cutting, iron-fisted control, and regulation, then what does leadership look like?

While management is about regulating people, leadership is about building relationships with people. This starts out with respect. Northouse posits, "Leaders are not above or better than their followers."[5] Leaders need some time alone to plan and reflect; if this causes them to be isolated for long periods of time, they should make a conscious effort to have meaningful interactions with the people they work with and who ultimately determine the success of the students' education.

Building relationships and showing respect are important foundations for leadership. But Louis Farrakhan, in his frequent writings about leadership, takes it a step further. Elijah Muhammad once said, "My mission is to give life to the dead,"[6] meaning proper knowledge will awaken in people a consciousness about themselves and will inspire them to find a purpose for living. Farrakhan likewise sees leadership as the ability to draw out in others their potential and to help them discover their divine essence.

At the core of Farrakhan's ideas about leadership is love. He once said, "The greatest characteristic that a leader must have is a four-letter word: Love. Because it's only love of the people that puts their worth and value above your own! It's love of the people that will put their lives above your own." Farrakhan is echoing the words of Jesus who declared, "Greater love has no man than he lay down his life for his friends." Those aspiring to leadership roles should reflect on the depth of their love for the people they are leading.

He contrasts this emphasis on love and sacrifice with what we often think of as leadership. In 2012, he wrote,

> "Leadership" is undergirded by a Divine Principle. Some of us think that "good looks" make us "good leaders," and maybe that's why we're in the shape that we're in. "Leadership" is not for the arrogant. Some of us think that "great articulation of words" and "beautiful speech" is what makes "good leaders," and maybe that's why we're in the condition that we're in, because we always choose leaders that can speak well, but don't do well. And we always choose leaders sometimes that appeal to our fancy of what "leadership" is without ever considering the Divine Principle that undergirds real, and true, leadership.[7]

For Farrakhan, leadership is rooted in the Corinthians, chapter 13, verse 4: "Love is patient, love is kind. It does not envy, it does not boast, it is not proud. It does not dishonor others, it is not self-seeking, it is not easily angered, it keeps no record of wrongs. Love does not delight in evil but rejoices with the truth. It always protects, always trusts, always hopes, always perseveres."

If you were to replace the *love* with *leadership* it would read as such: "Leadership is patient, leadership is kind. It does not envy, it does not boast, it is not proud. It does not dishonor others, it is not self-seeking, it is not easily angered, it keeps no record of wrongs. Leadership does not delight in evil but rejoices with the truth. It always protects, always trusts, always hopes, always perseveres." Out of the idea that love is leadership other principles emerge, such as *humility, listening, forgiveness, kindness, selflessness, truth,* and *perseverance*. Undergirding these is a certain knowledge that feeds intelligence that grows leaders into the practice of these principles.

HOW LOVING LEADERSHIP WORKS

Since leadership involves reaching or accomplishing a particular goal for educational leaders, the purpose of education becomes essential. Educational leaders who see the goal of education as meeting the human capitalist ideology that reinforces high-stakes testing, punitive disciplinary policies, and other unjust polices might be unconcerned with the concept of love. Educational leaders working from a human capitalist ideology will more than likely act as transactional leaders. *Transactional leadership* "refers to the bulk of leadership models, which focus on the exchanges that occur between leaders and their followers."[8]

An example of transactional leadership would be teachers receiving merit pay for increased test scores. Opposite to transactional leaders are those educational leaders who see education as the process of transforming human life. Those leaders will be more inclined to embrace love as an essential principle for leadership.

Transforming human life through education might be similar to the stages that a caterpillar goes through, only to become a butterfly. It is a metamorphosis into something new, unique, beautiful, and free. Seeing transformation as a goal of education could be likened to a *cloud* (leader/teacher) traveling over a *dead earth* (people/students). As the cloud begins to drop water on the earth, it begins to bring life to a dead earth. The heaven/earth relationship is a powerful sign of love. And like the heaven/earth relationship, when educators begin to rain love (knowledge) on the students and school community, what emerges is a new form of life.

Most educational leaders never use the term *love,* and in the context of leadership, the term can conjure or draw blank stares. Traditionally leadership has resembled authoritarianism. But Farrakhan advocates love, not as a touchy-feely emotion but as the creative force that the Creator used to begin creation: "I am talking about that creative force out of which the Almighty God Allah created the universe."[9] So for educational leaders, the concept of love means being able to organize and develop a culture that produces life. Love is not an emotion; it is an action, a verb, through which life is produced.

Life is based on the principles of freedom, justice, and equality. When educational leaders think about love, they should think about an environment that promotes these principles—and an environment that will stimulate the creative mind so that students can develop innovative ideas about how to pursue these principles throughout their lives. In this type of educational setting, teachers begin to develop lessons that bring out creative thinking from their students.

This means, for example, that when studying biology, students are encouraged to think about new ideas for curing cancer, however unorthodox. In this type of educational setting, principals could ask faculty to sit down for coffee, to explore ways that the leadership could better assist teachers in reaching their goals. In this type of setting, county administrators could listen to their principals' ideas for improvement with an open mind and an attitude of respect and possibility.

THE CHARACTER OF A LEADER

If leadership is influencing others through love, what are the specific characteristics that a leader should have to accomplish this? Love means bringing out the best in people. Jesus taught, "The good man brings out the good in people and the evil man brings out the evil in people." To bring out is a quality of leadership. In this section, we'll look at some of the characteristics of true leaders that allow them to bring out the best in others: forgiveness, empowerment, humility, listening, selflessness, perseverance, and intelligence.

Forgiveness

One underrated characteristic of true leaders is forgiveness—being willing to give people a pass when they make a small mistake and give them thoughtful, kind feedback when they make a large one. John Hoyle illustrated this when he described a secretary's first day at work, when she made some errors. After fearfully sharing with her supervisor the mistakes, her supervisor surprisingly responded, "This pencil has two ends: one for writing and one for erasing mistakes. Mistakes are part of the job: erase them and move on."[10]

No one wants to be belittled or hounded for small mistakes. And yet too many schools have a toxic environment that emerges from rigidity, judgmental attitudes, and an emphasis on control and regulation. Perhaps a classroom assistant, in a year of exemplary service, makes a small mistake because she didn't know of an obscure school rule. Maybe a teacher comments negatively on a principal's position on a particular issue, and news of it reaches the principal. When the small mistake ends up in a performance review, or the principal looks to punish her critic with scheduling or duties, resentment and anger start to fester.

Soon there is a culture where administrators are constantly at odds with the people in the organization. Every encounter becomes unpleasant. Principals feel beleaguered, and the staff feels unappreciated. Before long, in the place where people are supposed to be getting an education, they find themselves in a quagmire of dysfunction. Teachers and administrators find themselves thinking more about their unfair treatment than about their work. They stew and fixate on the perceived injustice, and they lose the creative impulse that should inform their teaching.

For all of these reasons, being able to forgive people for mistakes or personal attacks is a key hallmark of leadership. Being able to look past mistakes, rumor, and innuendos to see the greater purpose for being in the profession of education can help the leader to avoid the formation of toxic cultures that can permeate educational environments. Everyone makes mistakes, and treating them as a normal part of the work process bestows dignity on staff—a kind of dignity and understanding that they are then likely to extend to others.

Louis Farrakhan, himself the recipient of many verbal attacks, emphasized this when he wrote, "It is love of the people that will make you bear the insults of the people that you come to lead."[11] Love of students will be the key that allows educators to forgive and forget and to concentrate on their true mission.

Love and forgiveness are especially important traits when we are educating students who are members of a historically oppressed group. Sometimes persons from historically oppressed groups have a double consciousness within them whereby, on the one hand, they want freedom, and on the other, they are afraid of freedom. Paulo Freire, speaking about the fear of freedom, writes, "The oppressed having internalized the image of the oppressor and adopted his guidelines are fearful of freedom."[12] Farrakhan explains the necessity of love when leading historically oppressed people, saying, "Black people are difficult to lead, and if you don't have love, they will wear you out." All educators need forgiveness, and all students need to be forgiven when the going gets tough.

Empowerment

Leadership as love results in empowerment because it allows people to discover the leader within. In this sense, leaders who are in love with their followers are not threatened when they see their followers having success. We have all seen people in leadership positions become jealous of those they see as rising in greatness. And as a result of jealousy, they seek to stunt the rising leader's potential.

Farrakhan has spoken about the need for those in leadership positions to cultivate others to become leaders. When administrators set an example of joy in the success of others, teachers can begin to emulate this dynamic and find their own joy when students do well—and set an example for their students to do the same. Leadership gives birth to leadership. Love empowers people to maximize their full potential—and to find joy in their doing so.

Humility

One of the primary principles of leadership is humility. Farrakhan once wrote, "Humility has to be a characteristic of among leaders. We should not think more of ourselves than we should." Humility is rooted in the word *humus,* which means earth. Farrakhan described an experience where he was given the ashes of cremated person, and he placed these ashes on his desk to remind him "from dust I came and to dust I return." The ashes keep him humble and respectful of all life that exists.

Humility can be a challenge for educational leaders. They are often the highest paid in their school community, drive the finest cars, and have access to more resources than others. It's easy to become arrogant when such material discrepancies exist. Farrakhan described this temptation in 2012: "There is another most important characteristic that the leaders of this world do not have, which Jesus had with his Disciples: Big 'ego' problems. The Disciples wanted to have the uppermost seats in the building. . . . You know how pseudo leaders are? They come late, but, they want to come first! . . . These kinds of 'ego needs' start scratching you off for 'leadership.'"[13]

Humility has to be a characteristic among leaders. And you know how we are: we're so starved for "appreciation" and "ego gratification" that it's easy to succumb to the temptation to use leadership as a way to satisfy ego needs. This is false leadership. Authentic leadership means operating from a moral premise whereby the leader strives to do what is right. It also includes "knowing and acting on what is true in yourself, in your organization, and in the world."[14]

Authentic leaders do not necessarily seek leadership roles but find themselves developing relationships with people who thrust them into the leadership role. Northouse calls these *emerging leaders*: "The individual acquires emergent leadership through the people in the organization who support and accept that individual's behavior."[15] Emerging leaders have a uniqueness that is undergirded by love. And because they are not locked into the formal role of leadership, they have a type of influence that those who sit in formal leadership do not have because they may be tasked with conforming to policies that might not be in the best interest of those they lead.

Authentic leaders cannot easily be bought or sold for a price because of their commitment to those under their leadership. These authentic leaders do not see themselves as persons striving to become a university president, provost, dean, department chair, superintendent, or principal solely for the perks or monetary gains that come with the job. This is not to say that leaders should not be afforded these perks, because with leadership comes more responsibility, which means more stress and less personal time. However, authentic leaders do not sell out the people for monetary gain.

The story of Jesus when he was tempted by Satan demonstrates authentic leadership through the representation of agape love. *Agape* here means self-sacrificing love for God. An illustration of authentic leadership through agape love occurred when Jesus was led into wilderness, and while fasting for forty days and forty nights was tempted by Satan. Satan brought him to a high mountain and showed him all the kingdoms of the world and their glory.

Then he offered Jesus all of the kingdoms of the world if he bowed down and worshiped him. Imagine having ownership of all the wealth found in Africa, China, Russia, Brazil, Europe, and America at your disposal if you were to only give up your love of God. Jesus, remaining faithful to his mission to teach the good news that the kingdom of God was at hand, refused wealth to complete his mission.

In a like manner, educational leaders who see their positions as fulfilling a much higher calling would look for ways to resist those who are shaping educational policies that are preventing the people's growth from reaching its full potential. There is a need for educational leaders who are authentic and rooted in agape love. It is these types of leaders that will create a paradigm shift in education in the twenty-first century.

Farrakhan, cogently speaking to humility and leadership, says, "Humility is the quality or condition of being humble . . . it is a quality that a leader must have to lift up the weight of the people. The power of strength is in placing it under the weight. The leader cannot pull the people from above. The leader must get under and lift them up."[16]

Listening

Humility will lead to other important virtues for a true leader. A leader will understand that their occasional isolation means that they don't always see the challenges that people in the organization face on a daily basis. They will understand that their staff knows things that they, the administrators, don't know. And understanding this, they will actively seek opportunities to meet with their staff and *listen.*

Very few educational leaders take the time to sit with students, teachers, and community members to discuss how they feel. But listening to others is one of the most important parts of being a leader. In the Nation of Islam, one of the things that made Elijah Muhammad so successful was the table talks that he had with his followers. Louis Farrakhan continued this tradition, and during his table talks, he encourages participants to share their ideas, following up with questions and encouraging them to elaborate.

Listening to the people that you lead is a key component for effective leadership. Hunter writes, "Active listening requires a disciplined effort to silence all the internal conversation while we're attempting to listen to another human being. It requires sacrifice, an extension of ourselves, to block out the noise and truly enter another person's world—even for a few minutes."[17] This is a hard task that requires great self-discipline, but it's worth it.

Imagine what it would be like if the principal held table talks with the students who were the most troubled in the school, inviting them to have lunch in a place where both parties could share their concerns. This gives the leader the opportunity to enter the world of the troubled student and, like a doctor, begin to discover the remedy for the students' problems. Coming from a person who has formal authority, this might lead students who are considered troubled to find their way.

In similar fashion, the educational leader could do the same with other constituents such as teachers, staff, and community leaders. In the university setting, the president or provost might take time to break bread with department chairs or students—and along the way hear about problems he didn't know about or solutions he had never thought of. This type of dedicated listening benefits everyone involved: the leader understands his organization better, and those he leads feel valued and empowered.

Selflessness

Those in leadership roles must recognize that with the role of leadership, there are certain kinds of problems. These problems or challenges that exist within the organization are—fairly or unfairly—usually attributed to the leader. If one examines schools and colleges whenever a problem emerges, the leader is usually called to respond, even if they had nothing to do with the situation. Sometimes administrators are removed from their positions for situations they had no hand in creating.

These problems will often cause the leader to say it is either *me* or *them*. However, leaders should be reminded that these attacks are not necessarily an attack on the person but rather come with the territory of leadership. Thus, leaders have to become selfless, meaning losing more of their self-interest to invest in the interest of others. Selflessness means removing the personal, which removes *I* from leadership. They must put aside their natural concern for themselves to think more about the mission of the organization.

Perseverance

The number of demands that are placed on leaders can be very stressful. Every day they open their e-mail to find complaints and requests from students, faculty, parents, and upper administrations. While a good leader will put in place processes to avoid problems coming to a head and will create a command structure that allows his staff to handle many issues, there are times when those issues still find their way to the desk of the educational leader.

At any given moment, problems or issues can arise that the educational leader has not anticipated. The problems that can happen as a result of something going wrong can diminish the leader's will to continue. In higher education, the political climates that permeate these institutions often result in higher education administrators not staying in their positions for very long periods of time. Thus it becomes important for leaders to find a purpose and meaning to their work that extends beyond an appointed position. Thus they need to find alternative ways to lead people to the mountain of success that is outside of formal appointments.

For those educational leaders working in the academy, it behooves them to have a research agenda that speaks to the body of knowledge they are most interested in professing. Great leaders are teachers, and it is their ability to teach that makes them leaders, not a formal position. Perseverance is rooted in the concept that love endures. Love of students and knowledge will allow a leader to weather the temporary storms and still find a way to educate and inspire.

Intelligence

Ultimately, all leaders are only leaders for a certain amount of time. They can directly inspire while they are in their leadership position, but that influence only lasts as long as the job. What is important is that leaders share the knowledge and wisdom that they've accumulated with others in a way that will outlast their own tenure.

Knowledge isn't just the result of degrees and diplomas. Knowledge is the realization of our own worth and potential. We're two thousand years removed from the physical presence of Jesus and fourteen hundred years from the physical presence of Muhammad, but people continue to follow these great persons. In reality, it is not the physical person that we are following but it is the knowledge they brought that inspires us to face and overcome the challenges in our daily lives. Educational leaders need the same breadth and depth of knowledge so that they can inspire or breathe life into the people they lead.

Educational leaders today are faced with challenges like high-stakes testing and the need to improve test scores. A manager with conventional training may look at these challenges and think that students need more class time. A leader with wisdom, on the other hand, may see that in reality students might need more play time—to allow them to foster their creativity, enjoy learning, and feel free and capable. A leader will also understand the subjects that the students are expected to master, so that they can understand the stumbling blocks and challenges that each subject presents. By demonstrating comfort with these academic subjects, the leader also provides students with an example of mastery that can inspire them.

Louis Farrakhan emphasized knowledge in his writings on leadership and also provided a potent example of true leadership. He has taught and inspired a wide range of people, from spiritual leaders, teachers, coaches, and entertainers to drug dealers, killers, and more. He motivated nearly two million Black men to assemble in Washington, DC, for the Million Man March. To do such a thing, you have to know how to effectively reach a particular goal. Leadership must know where it is trying to go and also how to get there. The word *philosophy* comes from the Greek for "love of knowledge." You can't be a great leader without love for knowledge—the kind that shows others where they can go and how to get there.

CONCLUSION

The virtues discussed above are key to exercising leadership as love. Forgiveness allows staff to do their best with confidence and focus, without fear of undue reprisal. Empowerment gives them a voice—and encourages them to give their students a voice. Great leaders like Mohandas Gandhi, Nelson Mandela, Dr. Martin Luther King Jr., and Mother Theresa demonstrated humility—which, far from being a sign of weakness, actually demonstrates the leader's confidence that there is a higher calling behind their mission.

Listening allows leaders to understand the desires, needs, and challenges of those in the organization. Selflessness allows them to put the needs of their students first. Perseverance prepares them to weather the storms that always come with leadership. And intelligence allows them to pass on to others the knowledge that will outlast their own tenure and allow their students and teachers to achieve their goals.

Farrakhan points out that love is the creative force that brought all things into existence. And, once brought into existence, the law of freedom, justice, and equality are the principles that undergird love. The treating of those in the organization with dignity, respect, and compassion brings out the best in people, causing them to evolve through stage after stage until they have tapped the leader within. After discovering the leader within, they will be able to influence others to find their purpose for being in the organization. They will no longer go to work but go to purpose. And to find purpose is to discover love.

In the Bible, God appears to Solomon and asks him to disclose whatever he desired. In response to God's question Solomon declared, "Give me wisdom and knowledge, that I may lead this people, for who is able to govern this great people of yours?" For Louis Farrakhan, leadership begins with a request to God for wisdom and knowledge, but above all love. As he wrote,

> Look at the Principle that Jesus articulated: "Not my will, but Thy Will be done." So, to "worship God" and to "honor God" is one of the first Principles of Leadership! According to the Book, he said, "I"—pay attention to his words—"can of myself do nothing; whatsoever the Father bids me to do, that I do. And whatsoever the Father bids me to say, that I say." Do you know how powerful that is? When whatever God commands is what you do, and what you say? Have you noticed how people that are in leadership always use the personal pronoun "I," and they never get anything done because "I can of myself do nothing"? Only God has the right to say "I." But all of us: The principle is "we."[18]

Educational leaders in the twenty-first century will need to draw from spiritual knowledge to be effective leaders during these dynamic and tumultuous times in which we live.

NOTES

1. P. G. Northouse, *Leadership: Theory and Practice* (Thousand Oaks, CA: Sage, 2016), p. 5.
2. J. C. Maxwell, *Developing the Leader within You* (Nashville: Thomas Nelson, 1993), p. 1.
3. Peter Block, cited in John Hoyle, *Leadership and the Force of Love: Six Keys to Motivating People with Love* (Thousand Oaks, CA: Sage, 2002), p. 50.
4. Hoyle, *Leadership and the Force of Love*, p. 3.
5. Northouse, *Leadership*, p. 6.
6. Elijah Muhammad, *Message to the Blackman in America* (Chicago: Final Call, 1965), p. 306.
7. L. Farrakhan, "Principles and Practice on Leadership to Suffice Our Needs," *Final Call*, November 30, 2012, pp. 1–5.
8. Northouse, *Leadership*, p. 186.
9. Farrakhan, "Principles and Practice on Leadership."
10. Hoyle, *Leadership and the Force of Love*, p. 39.

11. Farrakhan, "Principles and Practice on Leadership."
12. P. Freire, *Pedagogy of the Oppressed* (New York: Continuum, 2000).
13. Farrakhan, "Principles and Practice on Leadership."
14. Northouse, *Leadership,* p. 255.
15. Northouse, *Leadership,* p. 8.
16. Farrakhan, "Principles and Practice on Leadership."
17. James Hunter, *The Servant: A Simple Story about the True Essence of Leadership* (New York: Crown Publishing Group, 2012), p. 105.
18. Farrakhan, "Principles and Practice on Leadership."

Chapter Three

Servant Leadership

The term *servant leadership* was coined by Robert Greenleaf and is the centerpiece of his world-renowned book of the same name.[1] Servant leadership is a conception of leadership that is grounded in the leader sufficing the needs of those in the organization. It is grounded in love, selfless actions, and behavior for the good of others and the organization. This chapter explores Louis Farrakhan's teachings on servant leadership and its application to the practice of educational leadership.

THE MEANING OF SERVANT LEADERSHIP

Robert Greenleaf coined the term *servant leadership* in the 1970s. In his definition of servant leadership, he wrote,

> Servant leadership begins with the natural feeling that one wants to serve, to serve first. Then conscious choice brings one to aspire to lead . . . the difference manifests itself in the care taken by the servant—first to make sure the people's highest priority needs are being served. The best test . . . is do those served grow as persons; do they, while being served, become healthier, wiser, freer, more autonomous, more likely themselves to become servants? And what is the effect on the least privileged in society; will they benefit, or, at least, will they not be further deprived?[2]

Farrakhan describes the principle of servant leadership in very similar terms:

> The Principle of Leadership is not based on "ego gratification." The Principle of Leadership is based on serving, and seeing that the people whom you're

serving value the service, benefit from the service and grow from the service; in order, then, that they become that to others as you have become that to them.[3]

These definitions are far from the traditional conception of leadership. For most, the leader is the boss, and the people in the organization serve the boss. Those schooled in this traditional conception may find it hard to embrace servant leadership. They may see it as debasing or robbing them of their authority and even privileges. Perhaps this is why most educational-preparation programs do not focus on servant leadership. Considering the numerous schools and colleges that are attended by historically underserved students, one would think that servant leadership would be one of the major areas of discourse.

Even when leaders embrace the concept of servanthood, they may find it hard to implement in daily practice. Some university administrators, for example, espouse the principle of servant leadership, but fail the test of actual servant behavior. They may micromanage the campus, fail to provide resources to middle-management administrators, and cut back on paying faculty for additional courses. They fail to honor and serve their faculty through resources, autonomy, and respect.

Farrakhan addressed the gulf between espousing a principle and acting on it in daily life:

> Now when "we serve," on the plate that you're serving your people must be The Answer—not to their "wants," but to their needs, because every human need is a human right. So when you look at your people and see their needs, then as a "leader" or "one who aspires to leadership," then you must examine your heart for "love," and examine your heart for "service."[4]

Servant leadership in this context means that the leader should serve the needs, not the wants, of those in the organization.

In an educational environment, what are some of the needs that students have in schools and universities? Servant leadership in the context of educational leadership can be explored through the lens of Maslow's hierarchy of human needs. According to Maslow, human needs are ordered in five layers. At the base, there are food, water, shelter; then safety and security; then belonging and love; then self-esteem; and finally self-actualization.

FOOD, WATER, SHELTER

In impoverished communities, one of the major problems that can be found is the lack of basic needs such as food, water, and shelter. Jonathan Kozol, in his book *Amazing Grace*, wrote about the horrendous conditions that inner-city youth live in.[5] Kozol followed these students to school and found that the school, like the community, was deplorable. While Kozol's study focused on inner-city schools, rural areas have similar problems with regard to basic health care and the physical facilities of the school. Educational leaders who are assigned to provide leadership in schools that experience *savage inequalities* often find themselves more focused on raising test scores than serving students' basic needs.

It's easy to think that schools do provide students with food, water, and shelter. Kozol, to the contrary, found that children in poor communities have terrible food choices. Unlike wealthier schools where the children have an abundance of healthy food choices, children in his study were offered more junk food and foods higher in calories and fat and lower in nutrients. With regard to shelter, some schools that poor children attend have rundown physical facilities, poor lighting, little in the way of modern technology, and may have no air conditioning in the hot months. The schools' physical appearance may be more like a prison than a school.

Charles Strange and James Banning, in their book *Educating By Design*, address the need for educational leaders to have knowledge of the psychological impact campus design has on student learning.[6] Good school design and a positive environment are not luxuries or niceties; they are essential to student learning and success. The school design does not only have an impact on the students but also on teachers as well. Hot classrooms, leaking roofs, and lack of supplies leave teachers frustrated, physically uncomfortable, and even exasperated at the amount of money they spend personally on supplies that the school doesn't offer. Almost any teacher outside of a wealthy district can tell you how much he or she spends out of pocket just to provide the basics for their classrooms.

So what is the servant leadership response to these conditions? Contrary to solely focusing on test scores, servant leaders would begin by trying to understand the communities that their students come from. Servant leaders might drive through the community in the late hours to see what's going on there that might have an influence on students. They may see families being evicted from their homes or kids out at night unattended. Such leaders will meet with community leaders to find out more about their community's challenges. They take the time to find out in which ways students' basic needs are being met or not met. Understanding the context that the student comes from is essential.

When leaders fully understand their communities, they can begin to pool the resources of the community. Every community has resources that can be harnessed for better schools. In schools where the physical facilities are in shambles, servant leaders could galvanize the human resources of the community to paint the buildings, repair broken restrooms, and beautify the outside of the campus through landscaping. They could draw up plans to improve food choices and fundraise for air-conditioning.

One core principle for Louis Farrakhan—and indeed the whole Nation of Islam from its beginning—has been autonomy, independence, and self-sufficiency. It is this do-for-self action plan that has made the Nation of Islam so successful in the Black community. From the start, the Nation of Islam built mosques and schools as beacons of order and pride in the heart of urban blight, representing life in the midst of death.

In Atlanta, the Nation of Islam's minister Abdul Sharrieff and Reverend Timothy Cole have applied the do-for-self spirit to galvanize the community to rebuild "the Bluff," the highest crime area in the state of Georgia. Through their efforts, the community has started pooling resources to clean the community up. The movement started in the community, and one of the local Home Depot stores got involved, donating not just paint but all supplies to improve homes in the area.[7]

Like other Nation of Islam leaders, Farrakhan has consistently urged Blacks to take control of the communities where they live. Educational leaders working in these environments have a model in the Nation of Islam that can be applied to the rebuilding of schools. It is important for servant leaders to not only focus on providing for their students' needs but also to believe that those needs can be met and to act to make this a reality. Farrakhan wrote,

> Leadership provides the needs of the people. Where Black people live in cities throughout America, there are food deserts. Once the people learn the value of good food, then as a leader, you want to be able to produce food—"if you're going to lead, you have to feed." Jesus fed The Multitude! Well, we might as well start! Feed yourself good health, but my point is: Leadership suffices needs.[8]

Servant leaders begin by exploring what the needs of the people are, and they work to suffice those needs. Certainly, the test-score frenzy that is being propagated does not serve a vital need for those suffering from the lack of good food, water, and shelter. Servant leaders in the context of schools might begin by thinking about a plan of action that ensures that students' basic needs are met. In doing so, these servant leaders create a world in the school that is different from the external world that students live in every day. Much like the mosque in a blighted neighborhood, the school can then provide an oasis of stability, health, and potential that will inspire students to aim high.

SAFETY AND SECURITY

In Maslow's hierarchy, the second most basic level of needs is safety and security. Teaching how to make communities safe for historically underserved communities has been one of the highlights of Minister Farrakhan's work as leader of the Nation of Islam. He has declared, "We have to make our own community a decent place to live and make it safe and habitable for our people."[9]

How do we make our schools safe and habitable for our students? The starting point for building safe school communities is the reorienting of students' thinking to take ownership of their school community. In the Nation of Islam, there are training classes for men and women. These training classes are called the Fruit of Islam for men and Muslim Girls Training Class for the women. One focus of these classes is the art of self-defense. Students in these classes are taught the martial arts, which trains them to defend their community. Working in cohesion or toward a common goal, they are given orders within this training that allows them to communicate effectively for the protection of their community.

Applying this type of training in schools would create unity among students and the larger school community. It would reduce gang violence, it would cause students to self-regulate, and it would reduce the vandalism that occurs in schools because the students would take ownership of the school. Their training would equip students with the skills and confidence to effectively deal with those trying to create a nuisance in the school.

Donna Gollnick and Phillip Chinn, in their widely read book *Multicultural Education in a Pluralistic Society*, discuss Louis Farrakhan and the Nation of Islam's work in transforming one of Washington, DC's worst communities: "Members have become visible role models in many inner cities as they establish businesses. They often serve as visible neighborhood guardians against crime and drug abuse, and have assumed an important role in the rehabilitation of individuals released from prison."[10]

In New Orleans, the Nation of Islam's minister Willie Muhammad incorporated a Squash the Beefs program that allows those who have disagreements to come together to resolve those differences. Imagine a Squash the Beef program in schools where violence is rampant. On a daily basis, there are conflicts that occur in schools, and a program like Squash the Beef could go a long way in eradicating these problems in school.[11]

Farrakhan and the Nation of Islam offer a model of how schools and their surrounding communities can be made safe. It involves taking ownership of the environment and believing that leaders and students can make a difference. When students feel secure and unafraid, it frees them to concentrate on education. A true servant leader will look at this need and find ways to make sure it is being met.

BELONGING AND LOVE

Most people attend school for at least twelve years and spend more time in school than at home. So when we look at rates of criminality in poor communities, we have to look at the influence of schools in addition to home and neighborhood. In a conversation with a group of principals,[12] they were asked who has more influence on students: the principal or gang leaders. The principals replied that the gang leaders had more influence. As they began to walk through the reasons why gang leaders have more influence on students, they arrived at the conclusion that it was principals' lack of meaningful interaction with students that contributed to this situation.

A good illustration regarding the influence of gang leaders is this: A student who has very few resources is walking to school, and one of the gang leaders beckons him to come over. "Hey young homie, come holler at me for few minutes. What's up with you? I noticed you got some twisted shoes on. Look, I am going to give you a hundred to get you something to wear. I see you headed to school—let me drop you off."

The student then gets dropped off at the school in a Mercedes Benz. The other students watch as he gets out of the car, and instantaneously he becomes popular among the students at the school. However, when he walks into the school, he meets the principal, who does not even greet him but just walks past him as though he is invisible. When he enters his first class, the teacher just shakes her head and reminds him that he's still not passing in English. Later in the day, he goes to his PE class and is told by the teacher that he hasn't been dressing out for class and is wearing messed-up shoes. "You just seem like you wasting time in school."

In this scenario, who provided the student with a sense of care and belonging? Not the school. It's well known that gangs provide young people with a sense of belonging and camaraderie, and this is a crucial human need according to Maslow. If educational leaders want to have influence on young people, they must meet this need. Servant leaders see their role as serving their students. They create a culture where everyone is valued. They speak to the least of these students by inspiring all of those in the organization to belong and feel loved. The Nation of Islam has always employed the terms *brother* and *sister* to indicate their commitment and love toward others. This is the kind of commitment that students long to feel.

In the above scenario, if the student walked into school where the practice of servant leadership was applied, the following would happen: The principal sees Rakim entering the school and begins by saying, "Hey, how is it going, Rakim? Is everything all right with you? When you have a chance let's sit down for a few minutes. We need to start thinking about what you are going to do once you are finished with school. In fact, Rakim, I would like for you to participate in the field trip to State University."

In the first-hour class, the English teacher might say, "Rakim, you doing all right today. Your grades are not the best, but I know you can do better. We are going to have some orange juice and donuts one morning and talk about how you are going to get an A out of this course." In the PE class, the teacher might say, "Rakim, you have not been dressing out. What's going on with you? The reason I am asking is because I see greatness in you that is not being tapped."

Servant leaders make people in the school community feel a sense of belonging and loved. Imagine a university president or college dean who walks by the person who is cleaning the buildings without saying a word. Sometimes leaders overlook and devalue people in the organization who do not hold a title, and as a result these leaders create a culture where people do not feel as though they belong, nor do they feel loved. That's why Louis Farrakhan has said that those in leadership need to check their egos. The ability to make people feel loved was one of the great attributes that the prophets and great teachers exhibited. It was their practice of love that caused people to want to be in their presence.

In educational organizations, the students and staff often do not have a desire to be around the leaders because they operate from power—meaning that they use their *position* rather than their *influence* to get people to move toward a common goal. But position and power can only take people so far. To get others to follow and achieve great things, leaders must serve their students' and staff's need for belonging and love.

SELF-ESTEEM

Developing self-esteem in students is one of the areas in which schools do not thrive. Many have derided schools' penchant for giving out participation awards and praising a select group of students for just showing up. But real self-esteem doesn't come from words of praise alone. Nor does it come from standardized test scores or schools that process students like a factory would. It certainly doesn't come from a curriculum that is geared toward churning out compliant workers or that contains seeds of racism and White supremacy. It comes from achievement—and from teachers' belief that students *can* achieve. And from a curriculum that excites students' passions and thirst for knowledge.

For servant leaders, it's important to understand how knowledge, power, and self-esteem interact. They need to explore how curricula can diminish or ignite the desire for more knowledge. Components such as culturally responsive pedagogy align with servant leadership. Culturally responsive pedagogy begins with the students and then connects to the academic knowledge that is prescribed, causing students to see the relationships between their own experiences to that of the academic knowledge.

Freire saw value in the students having voice, and during his time working with oppressed groups, noticed that proper education could instill within them high self-esteem. This became the basis for his book *Pedagogy of the Oppressed* where he writes, "Knowledge emerges only through invention and reinvention, through the restless, impatient, continuing, hopeful inquiry human beings pursue in the world, with the world, and with each other."[13]

Like these educators, the Nation of Islam, through its many writings, inculcates in the student high self-esteem, making them realize their divine essence. Farrakhan succinctly says, "School is not school—it is the Steward of the Life Force in your and my children. It is the 'other Mother,' the other nurturer and fosterer of this child and its development on the road to its meeting with God."[14]

Building self-esteem starts with an expectation that the student has a jewel within that has to be cultivated. The role of teachers is to bring that jewel to the forefront of the student's consciousness and convey that the student has the potential to cultivate it. Once brought forth, the student begins to see what their purpose is in life. Farrakhan's educational philosophy is that God has given each person an aim and a purpose. As students begin to understand themselves, they realize their potential and their self-esteem is higher.

Self-esteem is one of the higher needs in Maslow's hierarchy, but it is the one that allows students to cultivate the "divine essence," as Farrakhan called it. To be a true servant leader, administrators and teachers must provide for this need in their students.

SELF-ACTUALIZATION

In Maslow's hierarchy of needs, self-actualization is the top-most level on the pyramid. Self-actualization is the ability to reach one's highest potential. Carl Rogers expresses this as "man's tendency to actualize himself, to become his potentialities . . . to express and activate all the capacities of the organism."[15]

Although self-actualization is the highest (thus least basic) of Maslow's needs, its influence redoubles down to all other needs. For example, self-actualization brings benefits to safety. How do you make the schools safe and secure? In his study guide titled "Self-Improvement—The Basis for Community Development," Farrakhan points out that constructing better buildings is only the start. Unless human beings are developed, they will destroy the magnificent buildings they make:

> Now there are many, many developers who buy land and develop that land into communities, towns, and cities, placing on this land magnificent structures costing hundreds of millions, even billions of dollars. This activity of land development is going on in Phoenix and in cities around this country, and indeed around the Earth. However, to those who spend those hundreds of millions and billions of dollars building structures, unless we build people, unless the human potential of people is developed then man in his underdeveloped state will ultimately destroy magnificent buildings that he has erected, and destroy the cities that he has built because of revolution and war.[16]

How does a servant leader support the self-actualization needs of their students? First of all, a servant leader will attend to the lower-level needs. Once the more basic needs are provided—food, shelter, safety, love, and so on—students are free to develop the crucial ability to realize their highest potential. This self-actualization depends on several important elements: *knowledge, self-control, opportunity,* and *perseverance through adversity.*

Reaching the goal of self-actualization involves transformation of the human being through the acquisition of *knowledge*. This could be in part why the Nation of Islam does not allow its members to partake in vices such as alcohol and drug use. Participating in these activities impairs the mind and deafens the inner voice. When humans begin to feed themselves mental junk, it weakens the mind and limits their potential. Of course, to avoid alcohol and drug use, students need to make the right choices. And *self-control* is what allows students to make the right choices.

Servant leaders in educational institutions should also provide students and staff *opportunities* to display their talents and gifts. In the high school setting students might display artistic drawings at national competitions, become involved in debate clubs, develop new technology for a science fair, or participate in a rap competition. Often, school is the only place where students can participate in these activities or have the opportunity to develop these specialized skills. When school becomes a place of opportunity and self-actualization, students will be drawn to school, and principals will have a fighting chance to compete with gangs for influence in their lives.

Another key to self-actualization is *perseverance through adversity.* All progress has moments of forward momentum and moments that feel like you're stalled. But, as Farrakhan has stated, human beings should be involved in a process where they are constantly evolving. Evolution occurs through struggle: "We must struggle in order to obtain our ultimate goal. Our ultimate goal is to meet with Allah [God]. Difficulty is an essential factor in the journey from being a speck of dust to being one with Allah [God]."[17]

CONCLUSION

When the patriarch of the Nation of Islam, Elijah Muhammad, wrote that his goal was to raise Blacks in America from the dead, this is what he meant: to raise them to a new level of consciousness that would awaken in them their divine essence. It is not enough to simply churn out workers or generate good scores on standardized tests. Servant leaders will devote themselves to drawing out their students' highest potential and teaching students to cultivate that jewel within.

NOTES

1. Robert K. Greenleaf, *Servant Leadership: A Journey into the Nature of Legitimate Power and Greatness* (New York: Paulist Press, 1977).
2. Robert K. Greenleaf, *Servant Leadership: A Journey into the Nature of Legitimate Power and Greatness*, 25th anniversary edition. (New York: Paulist Press, 2002), p. 15.
3. Louis Farrakhan, "Principles and Practices of Leadership to Suffice Our Needs," *Final Call*, November 30, 2012.
4. Farrakhan, "Principles and Practices of Leadership to Suffice Our Needs."
5. Jonathan Kozol, *Amazing Grace: The Lives of Children and the Conscience of a Nation* (New York: Crown, 1995).
6. C. Carney Strange and James H. Banning, *Educating By Design: Creating Campus Learning Environments That Work* (San Francisco: Jossey-Bass, 2001).
7. Richard Muhammad, Eric Muhammad, and Kenetta Muhammad, "Rebuilding The 'Hood,'" *Final Call*, April 12, 2016.
8. Farrakhan. "Principles and Practices of Leadership to Suffice Our Needs."
9. Kenetta Muhammad, "Making Our Community a Decent Place to Live Day," *Final Call*, March 30, 2016.
10. Donna Gollnick and Phillip Chinn, *Multicultural Education in a Pluralistic Society*, 9th ed. (Boston: Pearson, 2013), p. 256.
11. Rhodesia Muhammad, "Squashing 'Beefs' City By City with Conflict Resolution," *Final Call*, April 20, 2016.
12. Abul Pitre, personal communication, 2009.
13. P. Freire, *Pedagogy of the Oppressed* (New York: Continuum, 2000), p. 72.
14. L. Farrakhan, Self-Improvement Study Guides—"Self-Improvement: The Basis for Community Development," The Farrakhan Factor (website), http://www.farrakhanfactor.com/library/study_guides/self_improvement.html, p. 15.
15. Carl Rogers, *On Becoming a Person: A Therapist's View of Psychotherapy* (Boston: Houghton Mifflin, 1961), pp. 350–51.
16. Farrakhan, Self-Improvement Study Guides—"Self-Improvement," p.2.
17. L. Farrakhan, Self-Improvement Study Guides—Study Guide 3: "Overcoming Difficulty," The Farrakhan Factor (website), http://www.farrakhanfactor.com/library/study_guides/studyguide_03.html, p. 3.

Chapter Four

Transformative Leadership

Transformative leadership has become a popular buzzword in recent years. It is a concept grounded in critical educational theory and refers to leadership that is concerned about social justice and education as liberation. This chapter explores Louis Farrakhan in the context of critical educational theory, applying these concepts to transformative leadership.

WHAT IS TRANSFORMATIVE LEADERSHIP?

Carolyn Shields defines transformative leadership this way: "Transformative leadership discourses derive from a critical tradition, promoting emancipatory pedagogies that arise from political and social movements, and critical pedagogy."[1] The concepts in transformative leadership involve addressing inequities that exists in society and leadership for social justice. Carolyn Shields makes a distinction between transformative and transformational leadership, two expressions that are close enough to be confused but that are quite different in meaning. *Transformational leadership* means getting individuals in the organization intrinsically involved, whereas *transformative leadership* has the goal of social transformation.

Critical pedagogy "provides historical, cultural, political, and ethical direction for those in education who still dare to hope."[2] Grounded in a critique of education from historical, cultural, and political viewpoints, critical pedagogy offers the possibility of helping educational leaders become conscious of the inner workings of these institutions and their impact on students in relation to the larger society. It offers leaders the opportunity to understand how education is a political activity that works in the best interest of the powerful.

Critical pedagogy, while often described as having its origins in the Frankfurt school of thought, also has American origins that are grounded in the works of persons such as Martin Luther King Jr. and Malcolm X.[3]

While scholars in the Frankfurt School coined the term *critical* to refer to this kind of thinking, the role of power interests in education has long been a focus among Black leaders who offered compelling critiques of education and society. And unlike those who were from the Frankfurt School, they were the sons and daughters of slaves. The institution of slavery, by its design, mis-educated Blacks. It took away all vestiges of the greatness of Blacks by conveying an ideology that Whites were superior. For example, laws were passed that did not allow Blacks to read or pass on cultural values to their children. In fact, they were stripped of all vestiges of their culture.

Long before the advent of the Frankfurt School, Frederick Douglass wrote "What the Fourth of July Means to a Slave."[4] In this speech, Douglass offered a critique of American society, showing how the quintessential American holiday was not universally American at all. It offered to Whites the celebration of freedom and justice, while for Blacks it served only as a reminder of their continued slavery. Here Douglass engaged in an early example of critique, disclosing the elite-class interests that undergirded a seemingly universal phenomenon.

Douglass was not alone in his critique. Carter G. Woodson offered one of the most compelling critiques of Black education in his 1933 book *The Mis-Education of the Negro*. In fact, one could argue that Woodson's work laid the foundation for critical pedagogy. In *The Mis-Education of the Negro*, Woodson offered a trenchant look at the type of education Blacks were receiving.[5] He observed that Black education was in reality mis-education because it taught Blacks to despise everything African. After Woodson, came the likes of Elijah Muhammad, who followed the same lines of argument in *Message to The Blackman in America*. Elijah Muhammad attempted to reverse this mis-education by offering an alternative paradigm of Black identity in which the Blackman was the original man and his origin predated the sun, moon, and stars.[6]

In his lecture titled "The Origin of Blackness," Farrakhan asserted that the origin of Black people is in the universe out of which they came and goes on to describe how, when the first creator created himself, he took on the environment that birthed him.[7] Thus to be Black is not a curse; it is the state of the original human being in which all others have their origin. In detailing these origin stories, Muhammad and Farrakhan offered powerful critiques of White supremacy, rejected White mythologies of Black inferiority, and engaged in a potent form of transformative leadership.

BLACK LEADERS ON CRITICAL PEDAGOGY

Black intellectuals like Douglass and Woodson laid the foundation for *critical black pedagogy*. In examining the elements of traditional education for Black students, critical black pedagogy is grounded in four main constructs: *critical multicultural education, critical pedagogy, Afrocentricity,* and *African American spirituality*. It asks: What would schools and universities look like if Martin Luther King Jr. or Elijah Muhammad were leading them?

We have some idea of what they might look like because Elijah Muhammad not only critiqued traditional Black education but also organized a new system of education for Blacks. In the 1930s, he started the Muhammad University of Islam, a primary and secondary school in Detroit that eventually grew to a network of many schools across the United States. Elijah Muhammad has often been erased from the history of Black achievement and critical pedagogy; in fact, Louis Farrakhan, in a lecture titled "The Life and Times of Muhammad Ali," noted that in Chicago during Black History Month, teachers were told not to mention Elijah Muhammad or himself.[8] But Elijah Muhammad's achievement with the Muhammad University of Islam was one of the earliest implementations of critical black pedagogy.

The work of Elijah Muhammad and Louis Farrakhan has thus transcended critique and moved from theorizing to practice—the hallmark of transformative leadership. In the following sections, we'll look at the individual components of transformative leadership: challenging ideology, unmasking power, and overcoming alienation.

CHALLENGING IDEOLOGY

The Nation of Islam's implementation of transformative education has drawn criticism. Traditional educators are suspicious of critical pedagogy. Stephen Brookfield, writing about ideology, writes: "It describes the way people learn to accept as natural and in their best interest an unjust social order."[9] And he points out how critical theory challenges that understanding of the world: "Critical theory sees ideology as inherently duplicitous, as a system of false beliefs that justify practices and structures that keep people unknowingly in servitude."[10] Critical pedagogy thus challenges the White supremacist ideology that has been the foundation for keeping oppressed groups in servitude and offers a problematic threat to those in ruling positions.

It is important to note the comprehensive nature of Farrakhan's critical pedagogy. To effectively break the ideology of White supremacy, the true history of the diverse groups that make up American society should be taught in schools. This would develop a healthy respect for the various racial and ethnic groups, creating a more harmonious society.[11] It is not enough to simply include more diverse groups in the curriculum because, as seen in the prohibitions regarding Black History Month noted earlier, there is a tendency by those shaping the curriculum to construct it in ways that serve their interest.

Challenging ideology can be difficult because educational leaders are required to work within hierarchal educational structures that might perpetuate inequity. Educational leaders seeking to organize around principles that will liberate or make school communities conscious of these inequities could be in danger of losing their jobs. While there is a cadre of educational scholars who are focusing on issues of equity and social justice, the application of these principles can be difficult considering that schools are controlled by those with differing experiences. But doing so is critical to breaking the hegemony of White ideology in schools.

UNMASKING POWER

Another component of transformative leadership is the process of unmasking the power dynamics that operate under the surface of society and our schools. Critical race theorists argue that despite what appeared to be monumental changes for equity, equality, and social justice for Blacks in America, these changes only took place when they were really in the best interest of Whites. This phenomenon is called *interest-convergence*. Interest-convergence is the dynamic of change in which society only changes when it is in the interest of the dominant group to do so. Only when the interest of the dominant group becomes threatened will they change laws and policies.

For example, in 1954, *Brown v. Board of Education* charged schools with desegregating with all deliberate speed. This led to the dismantling of openly discriminatory practices, but it has taken several decades for historically underserved groups to attain some of the rights that are supposed to be granted through the U.S. Constitution. In addition, it can be argued that the dismantling of segregation served the interest of Whites more than it did Blacks in America. A good example is the enormous wealth that Black athletes are generating for predominantly White universities.

The idea of interest-convergence can also be seen in the sports world. Sports was once strictly segregated, but now Black athletes are bringing billions of dollars to majority White universities—while some historically Black colleges and universities are struggling for financial resources. The same dynamic can be seen in the entertainment field, where Black artists have proved to be profitable for non-Black owners of the media.

The advent of the modern athlete and the entertainment world that is bringing in trillions of dollars has also reshaped views about the White supremacist ideology that undergirds society. Daily on TV networks you can find Black anchors and cohosts narrating the sporting events. We have seen the election of the first Black president, and in many major urban areas, Black mayors and Black elected officials hold positions that could improve the living conditions of their constituents. Even in education, Blacks have been selected to serve as presidents of major predominantly White universities. This has created a small cadre of selected Black leaders who will argue that the problems occurring in Black communities are a direct result of their own doing.

But transformative leadership will unmask the power relations that still undergird our institutions. The virulent and open racism of the past has become more insidious and dangerous because it is cloaked in institutions through policies that perpetuate these inequities. This is certainly true in our educational institutions. Just as the criminal justice system criminalizes Black youth, schools participate in this criminalization through an overrepresentation of Black males in negatively labeled special education classes, with a higher number of expulsions and suspensions.

When queried about these challenges, both students and teachers respond that it is the result of coming from dysfunctional homes and communities. And while there is certainly no doubt that home life has an impact on student success, there are other factors that contribute to these problems. Freire cogently tackles this issue when he says that the oppressed could never initiate violence when they are shaped in violence: "Never in history has violence been initiated by the oppressed."[12]

Farrakhan provides a potent example of transformative leadership in this regard. He has pointed out how drugs, guns, and violence have been placed in the Black community. Through a process of social engineering, Black youth have been programmed for self-destruction: "Jails in America are being privatized, and they are on the stock exchange, and you don't build a hotel unless you expect occupancy. So when they are building prisons, they want to build them but they are building them for you. But now they have to create a culture in the community that leads to violence, crime, drugs, guns, prostitution and it's a steady pipeline to prison."[13]

Farrakhan takes the process of unmasking power a step further by disclosing the social engineers that are negatively influencing youth. If transformative leadership can disclose the way the powerful are engineering society, it can also unveil how groups that have been oppressed have the power to redirect their lives. The Nation of Islam's do-for-self philosophy has long advocated concrete steps to dismantle the hold that a ruling elite has on Black communities, emphasizing that the unity of the oppressed is more powerful than an atomic bomb.

J. Edgar Hoover ran a counterintelligence program in the 1960s directed at destroying Black organizations and ferreting out any potential Black "messiah" who could bring the diverse elements of the Black community into one single group. Years later, in 1995, Farrakhan's Million Man March demonstrated the awesome power of unity that could be generated among Blacks in America. At the march, Farrakhan urged Blacks to take ownership of their communities, through education (especially in agriculture), land ownership, and the pooling of resources to support historically Black colleges and universities.

OVERCOMING ALIENATION

A third component of transformational leadership is overcoming alienation. Brookfield writes, "we are alienated, in Marx's view, when we work and live in ways that estrange us from who really are."[14] To overcome alienation requires one to know or discover their purpose. Farrakhan writes, "Happiness comes when a person understands their purpose for existence and they fulfill that purpose."[15]

He argues that the current educational system is designed to alienate people from discovering their potential because it has been designed to produce workers: "You look at your life—you work if you have a job, but that is not what you are born to do. You do it out of necessity because there is a salary at the end of the week that allows you to pay the car note, the mortgage, go to the grocery store and feed yourself. . . . That is a slave existence."[16] Farrakhan's call for Blacks to find their true purpose in life is echoed in Brookfield's definition of individuals overcoming alienation by opening themselves to their creative powers: "By implication the removal of alienation allows for the possibility of freedom, for the un-manipulated exercise of one's creative powers."[17]

Transformative leadership when applied in the schools frees the people in the school community because it centers education on the discovery of one's powers. Unlike the traditional leadership that focuses more on following the managerial procedures, transformative leadership seeks to eradicate inequities. This involves a threefold process: challenging White ideology, unmasking power relations, and overcoming alienation by putting students in touch with their creative powers and sense of purpose.

BENCHMARKS FOR TRANSFORMATIVE EDUCATIONAL LEADERSHIP

A framework for dismantling inequities for transformative leaders might include Bank's multicultural benchmarks. Banks identified seven areas for leaders to concentrate on in order to put transformative leadership into concrete practice: *multicultural education policy statement, staff attitudes, curriculum, teaching strategies, school staff, parent participation*, and *teaching materials*.[18]

Multicultural Education Policy Statement

Educational leaders are charged with developing a shared vision. The vision and mission of the school or university provide it with core values that undergird everything that takes place. It is the shared vision that is the beginning point for leadership because it applies Northouse's concept of influencing people to achieve a common goal. The fuel for vision is knowledge. Transformative leaders skillfully share with the school community knowledge that awakens them to the deeper reason for being in the practice of educating.

Transformative leaders support professional development that grounds the school community in meaning and purpose and also critiques current practices that may be alienating those most marginalized in the school community. Transformative leaders facilitate the development of a mission statement that speaks to issues of equity, diversity, and social justice.

Staff Attitudes

Transformative leaders work to develop within their faculty dispositions that allow them to treat everyone in the organization with dignity and respect. When exploring the overrepresentation of Black males in special education, they may visit the classroom to see how teachers are interacting with Black male students. Moreover, they may sit with teachers to get their perspective about the overrepresentation of Black males in special education.

One study found that Black males, once placed in special education, were locked into a future with limited possibilities.[19] During the study, Black male students disclosed that being in special education destroyed their self-esteem. The students reported feeling as though they were in prison. And according to the study, these students had big dreams of doing something with their lives only to find that their placement in special education had destroyed their aspirations for greatness. They felt humiliated and dehumanized to the degree that they began to internalize negative self-concepts. Transformative leaders would work to prevent this from occurring through a careful study of staff attitudes.

Curriculum

At the heart of educating is the curriculum. The curriculum is the starting pointing for either domesticating or liberating students. Joel Spring, writing about the discourse on education, highlights this, asking, "What knowledge is most worth teaching?"[20] Apple, speaking to curriculum, points out that knowledge used in school is prescribed by those in power.[21]

Farrakhan also has written about traditional education systems noting the hiding of knowledge that keeps the oppressed in the inferior status. Speaking to the prescribing of knowledge, he discussed Woodrow Wilson's comments regarding the type of education the masses should receive: "We want a class of persons to have a liberal education and we want another class of persons, a very much larger class, of necessity, to forgo the privilege of a liberal education and fit themselves to perform specific difficult manual tasks."[22]

The curriculum is the foundation for preparing people for the roles that Wilson envisioned. Farrakhan recognized this, saying, "You have an educational system set up to make the mass into workers for the class."[23]

For Farrakhan, challenging the curriculum is a spiritual battle. Transformative leaders must critique the curriculum to assess how it meets the needs of their students. The current curriculum design and the way schools operate eliminate the awakening of the inner voice. The shift now is to make a common-core curriculum that can be transferred across state lines. Apple, writing as early as 1996, described a common-core type of curriculum that spat out conforming students like cheap French fries. Transformative leadership would challenge the current approach of using the curriculum as a form of social control.

Transformative leaders could organize professional-development opportunities that help teachers critique the prescribed curriculum. In so doing, the transformative leader would more than likely turn a blind eye to the pacing guides that have been used to deskill teachers and have caused students to become uninterested in learning. The transformative leader to some degree plays a dual role: to the school hierarchy and district administrators, he or she must give the appearance that everything is going according to the prescribed plan; alongside this, however, he or she must endeavor to make changes to the curriculum that will excite the imagination of students. The transformative leader looks for ways to create out-of-school experiences that include knowledge that is not in the prescribed curriculum.

At the university level, an examination of the curriculum is very disheartening. For example, the majority of universities offering PhDs in African American studies are predominately White universities. Another example is the course offerings in educational leadership programs at historically Black colleges and universities. Noticeably absent from their programs is a focus on leadership for social justice, with virtually no classes in the area of critical educational theory. Since the curriculum is the heartbeat of the school or university, the urgency to provide transformative curricula is pressing. For oppressed groups, the curriculum should bring about a consciousness that equips them to work for social change.

Jean Anyon, in her 1980 study "Social Class and the Hidden Curriculum of Work," identified four types of schools. Those schools included *working class schools*, *middle class schools*, *affluent schools*, and *executive elite schools*.[24] She noted that the hidden curriculum prepared some students for work and others for leadership. Anyon's ethnographic study in the K–12 setting may perhaps apply to colleges and universities.

Top-tier universities offer a robust curriculum, whereas other schools offer traditional courses. For example, one Ivy League university offered a course titled "The Nation of Islam" and there are several major universities that offer a course titled "Martin and Malcolm." In historically Black colleges and universities, the curriculum is often sanitized to be less threatening to those who fund them.

Elijah Muhammad once cited a U.S. senator regarding the need to appropriate money for Howard University; Muhammad stated, "What would be the need of the government appropriating money to educate Negroes? He [the senator] said that they would not teach our people the science of modern warfare, birth control or chemistry."[25] In other words, the curriculum would be prescribed in a way that would keep Blacks from being empowered. Muhammad goes on to say, "This shows the slave master has been very successful in dominating us with an education beneficial to him."[26]

Transformative leaders will be aware of the many ways that curriculum can undermine true education and perpetuate White supremacist ideology. When making changes to the curriculum, they can evaluate their progress in terms of Banks's four approaches to multicultural reform:[27]

- **Level 1: The Contributions Approach.** This approach focuses on heroes, holidays, and discrete cultural elements.
- **Level 2: The Additive Approach.** Content, concepts, themes, and perspectives are added to the curriculum without changing its structure.
- **Level 3: The Transformation Approach.** The structure of the curriculum is changed to enable students to view concepts, issues, events, and themes from the perspective of diverse ethnic groups.
- **Level 4: The Social Action Approach.** Students make decisions on important social issues and take actions to help solve them.

The goal for transformative leaders should be to align the curriculum in such a way that it reflects levels 3 and 4.

Teaching Strategies

Teaching strategies in schools is very important for transformative leaders. Nieto and Bode, in *Affirming Diversity: The Sociopolitical Context of Multicultural Education*, point out the discrepancy in teaching strategies for students in working-class schools.[28] They point out that the strategy used in urban schools is a *pedagogy of poverty* "that encompasses a body of specific strategies that are limited to asking questions, giving directions, making assignments, and monitoring seatwork."[29] This type of pedagogy is boring to students and takes away the desire to be in school. Farrakhan points out that schools should be places where students are having fun: "If it's not fun why would they want to be there?"

Transformative leaders might explore culturally responsive pedagogy as one method of helping teachers excite the imagination of students. Culturally responsive pedagogy involves connecting academic knowledge to the students' cultural backgrounds. Through culturally responsive pedagogy, students at the highest level are able to use their knowledge to work toward equity and justice.

School Staff

The majority of teachers are White females who often have very different experiences from the students they teach. Christine Sleeter argues that having a majority White teaching force matters: "Teacher race does matter, and for reasons that include and extend beyond issues of cultural congruence in the classroom."[30]

For transformative leaders, a major goal should be to recruit teachers from diverse backgrounds. However it is important to keep in mind that teachers should undergo professional development in the sociopolitical context of education. Kunjufu emphasizes that race is not the only issue affecting teacher demographics. There is also the issue of class: many teachers come from middle-class backgrounds, which distorts their view of non-mainstream students.[31]

Parent Participation

Transformative leaders should also attend to engaging diverse parents in the school community. This might include offering opportunities that extend past the regular work week to activities that could occur on the weekend. In addition, visiting churches and other community venues could provide opportunities for educational leaders to engage parents.

When queried about parent participation, educational leaders often talk about the lack of parental involvement of parents with lower socioeconomic status. Using a cultural-deficit perspective, these educational leaders never realize that the school may contribute to what is perceived of as a lack of parental involvement. For example, schools may not be welcoming to parents when they visit. In an observation of one school, the parents were waiting in the administrative offices for several minutes before anyone greeted them.

And while waiting, one parent asked if there was a restroom and was told there were no available restrooms on the campus.[32]

Here again, class and cultural capital matter. Parents with wealth or high class status have more privileges than parents with little cultural capital. In a school where the staff perceives parents to have cultural capital, where parents are doctors, lawyers, and even school board members, it is much more likely that restrooms would be offered for use. These small confrontations and insults have a heavy influence on how comfortable parents feel visiting schools and becoming involved in their children's education.

Teaching Materials

Transformative educational leaders should examine the materials that are being used in a classroom to ensure that they reflect the diversity of students in the class. On one occasion, a teacher had students read biographies of famous people. During the first five months, all of the biography subjects were White, despite the fact that there were ten Black students and only five White students in the class. In January, one of the Black students challenged the teacher, asking if at any point they were going to read about famous Black persons. The teacher never realized the impact this was having on her students. She was unknowingly reinforcing a White supremacist perspective on to her students.

CONCLUSION

Educational leaders in the twenty-first century will have numerous challenges. As schools become more bureaucratic, more politicized, and more market oriented, educational leaders will need the knowledge embedded in transformative leadership to be truly effective. It will be challenging for transformative leaders because more than likely they may be diametrically opposed to the human capitalist ideology that is driving school policies and practices. However, these leaders should take courage in knowing that change has always occurred through the sacrifices of persons willing to speak truth to power.

Farrakhan's educational philosophy is an important building block for transformative leadership. His insights into challenging ideology, unmasking power, and overcoming alienation can be the starting point for teacher-preparation programs to incorporate critical pedagogy in their curriculum. And his leadership in developing the Muhammad University of Islam can point the way for educators to move from theory to concrete practice.

NOTES

1. Carolyn Shields, *Transformative Leadership: A Reader* (New York: Peter Lang, 2011), p. 21.
2. Peter McLaren, *Life in Schools: An Introduction to Critical Pedagogy in the Foundations of Education*, 6th ed. (Boulder, CO: Paradigm, 2015), p. 122.
3. Michael Apple, Wayne Au, and Luis Gandin, eds., *The Routledge International Handbook of Critical Education* (New York: Routledge, 2009); P. McLaren, *Life in Schools: An Introduction to Critical Pedagogy in the Foundations of Education*, 6th ed. (Boulder, CO: Paradigm, 2015).
4. Dave Zirin, "What to the Slave Is the Fourth of July." *The Nation*, July 4, 2012.
5. Carter G. Woodson, *The Mis-Education of the Negro* (Chicago: African American Images, 1933).
6. Elijah Muhammad, *Message to the Blackman in America* (Chicago: Final Call, 1965).
7. L. Farrakhan, *The Education Challenge: A New Educational Paradigm for the 21st Century*. (Chicago: Final Call, 2009).
8. L. Farrakhan, "The Life and Times of Muhammad Ali," lecture delivered June 12, 2016, at Mosque Maryam at the Nation of Islam's National Center, Chicago, https://www.noi.org/muhammad-ali/.
9. Stephen Brookfield, *The Power of Critical Theory: Liberating Adult Learning and Teaching* (San Francisco: Jossey-Bass, 2005), p. 43.
10. Brookfield, *The Power of Critical Theory*, p. 40.
11. L. Farrakhan, *Torchlight for America* (Chicago: Final Call, 1993).
12. P. Freire, *Pedagogy of the Oppressed* (New York: Continuum, 2000).
13. L. Farrakhan, "Louis Farrakhan Exposes Rothschild Bankers" [video], lecture delivered on Savior's Day 1995, available at https://www.youtube.com/watch?v=_mAwjQpOalM.
14. Brookfield, *The Power of Critical Theory*, p. 49.
15. Farrakhan, *The Education Challenge*, p. 16.
16. Farrakhan, *The Education Challenge*, p. 17.
17. Brookfield, *The Power of Critical Theory*, p. 50.
18. J. A. Banks, *An Introduction to Multicultural Education* (Upper Saddle River, NJ: Pearson, 2014).
19. Esrom Pitre, *Locked In: African American Males in Special Education* (New York: Linus Publications, 2011).
20. Joel Spring, *The Politics of American Education* (New York: Routledge, 2011), p. 16.
21. Micheal Apple, *Ideology and Curriculum*, 2nd ed. (New York: Routledge, 2004).
22. Farrakhan, *The Education Challenge*, pp. 12–13.
23. Farrakhan, *The Education Challenge*, p. 13.
24. Jean Anyon, "Social Class and the Hidden Curriculum of Work," *Journal of Education* 162, no. 1, 1980, pp. 66–92.
25. Muhammad, *Message to the Blackman in America*, p. 40.
26. Muhammad, *Message to the Blackman in America*, p. 40.
27. Banks, *An Introduction to Multicultural Education*, p. 54.

28. S. Nieto and P. Bode, *Affirming Diversity: The Sociopolitical Context of Multicultural Education*, 6th ed. (Boston: Allyn & Bacon, 2012).

29. Nieto and Bode, *Affirming Diversity*, p. 124.

30. Christine Sleeter, "How White Teachers Construct Race," in *Race, Identity, and Representation in Education*, 2nd ed., ed. Cameron McCarthy et al., 243–56 (New York: Routledge, 2005).

31. Kwanza Kunjufu, *Black Students, Middle Class Teachers* (Chicago: African American Images, 2002).

32. Abul Pitre, personal communication, 2014.

Chapter Five

Futuristic Leadership

The societal crises that are impacting people across the globe raise concerns about leadership. The challenges confronting societies suggest the need for new ways of thinking about leadership in a world that is vastly different from the one in which many of the traditional practices of leadership were formed.

Margaret Wheatley, in her book *Finding Our Way: Leadership for Uncertain Times*, captures the challenges that leaders are facing in the twenty-first century.[1] In the field of education, these challenges include a new non-White majority in public schools, new forms of popular culture, religious diversity, new forms of technology, and cultural clashes in the United States and abroad. These challenges have often resulted in leaders using command-and-control leadership practices. Wheatley argues that these practices will not suffice for the times in which we live, causing her to advocate for a paradigm shift in leadership: "Leaders use control and imposition rather than self-organizing processes. They resort to uncertainty and chaos by tightening already feeble controls, rather than engaging our best capacities in the dance."[2]

At this critical juncture in American and world history, leadership is sorely needed to resolve these challenges. To embrace the new era, Wheatley contends that there is a need to look at indigenous ways of living to understand how to live in harmony with nature. Approaching the practice of leadership from the Western-centric perspective mechanizes the human being and does not tap their spirit. In the highly charged political climate, educational leaders are faced with resolving challenges that are found in the larger society.

While leadership theorists have offered numerous definitions of leadership, the majority concur that leadership is influence. This chapter explores leadership in the context of organizational development through the lens of human development and offers a new way of approaching the practice of leadership in the context of education. Drawing from Louis Farrakhan's teachings on organizational leadership, it explores what he sees as the core principles around organizing.

A NEW PARADIGM

Farrakhan has pointed out that human life has a predetermined goal, which is to become one with the Creator: "Before you came into existence there was a goal set for your life, and that goal is written of in the Bible and in the Quran, that goal is to make that life meet with its source, its creator."[3] Part of the purpose of education is to help human beings connect to the divine essence resonating in them. This divine essence is the inner voice that, once awakened and developed, becomes the leader within. The inner voice diminishes the need for an external leader because the person has now tapped the leader within. This is what Wheatley means when she talks of "self-organizing processes." Control will always be "feeble" unless it is developed from within.

Leadership is part of the education process that brings one into oneness with God. To discover the leader within aligns with Elijah Muhammad's teachings that he wanted to make Blacks self-rulers. When applied to the whole of humanity, it means that a new mind governs the human being, thus placing them on a new level of existence.

Leadership should serve the purpose of freeing people to discover the self. However, the current practice of leadership does not operate with the goal of freeing people. In fact, it could be argued that education leaders now are guiding students more toward a mentality of enslavement than liberation. Part of the process of enslaving involves an education process that *schools* rather than *educates,* as Mwalimu Shujaa argues in his book *Too Much Schooling, Too Little Education.*[4] Ivan Illich similarly asserted that school represents a way of getting people to conform to technocratic mechanisms that cause them to function as things.[5] Wheatley also comments that one of the problems that exist in organizations is that leaders do not allow for organizations to grow organically.[6]

Organizations often operate as machine-like structures and expect people to operate as machines. Wheatley goes on to say that machines do not have creativity, and one of the things that makes human beings unique is their ability to be creative. Creativity is found in living things that have the ability to self-create: "One of the most interesting definitions of life in modern biology is that something is considered alive if it has the capacity to create itself. The term for this is autopoiesis—self creation. Life begins from the desire to create something original, to bring a new being into form."[7] Wheatley is in consonance with Elijah Muhammad, who declared that the first God was self-created. He didn't pattern his creation on another but used his creative mind to bring into existence something that had not been created before. There is an organizing process at work in education now; however, that process is aborted because leaders attempt to mechanize a process that occurs naturally.

THE FUTURE OF ORGANIZATIONS

One of the reasons that educational leaders may resort to mechanizing their schools is that they do not have opportunities to think about leadership in the context of organization, particularly as it relates to bringing out creativity in human beings. This mechanistic approach to leadership might also be the result of what Ivan Illich (1976) describes in his book *Deschooling Society*, where he contends that schools are designed to produce automatons as opposed to human beings.[8] For Illich, society has to be *deschooled* because it has automated people to the degree that they are losing their humanity. Wheatley contends, "When we conceived of ourselves as machines, we must give up what is most essential to being human."[9] And too many educational leaders focus so much on the mechanistic side that they place themselves in positions where they are often found managing, not leading—that is, building relationship that stimulate creativity.

Organizational development and change is an important area of study for educational leaders. In the study of organizational development, one begins to explore how to develop the talent of individuals within the organization.[10] In addition to developing the people within the organization, areas such as culture and team building are emphasized. Anderson provides some excellent examples of organizations that do not thrive when its members do not feel valued; they find no purpose in the organization and do not feel free to be creative.[11]

Organizations that do not value people often have high turnover rates, or they become stagnant because the individuals in the organization do not perform to the best of their abilities. For educational leaders, it is important to study the culture of the organization and to engage in a process of introspection. Leaders need to question their motives for desiring to hold a leadership role: What are their philosophical views toward people? What are their views about the motivating factors of the people in the schools and universities they lead?

Believing in the Power of Purpose

McGregor, in his theory of human motivation, identified two theories that he named Theory X and Theory Y.[12] Theory X posits that people avoid work when possible and as a result need someone directing them through threats. Starmack, paraphrasing McGregor, writes, "Theory X works from the premises that people have an intrinsic dislike for work."[13] On the other hand, Theory Y contends that people will be committed to work if it is satisfying. With regard to Theory X, if it were rephrased in the following way, it would sound absurd: "Theory X works from the premises that people have an intrinsic dislike for purpose." By rephrasing or replacing *work* with *purpose*, one could argue that people in the organization would perform at the highest level.

In the educational setting, Theories X and Y can be seen in leadership expectations. Like teacher expectations, if educational leaders believe that the school community must be organized around threats and punishments to move toward a common goal, they will more than likely devalue the humanity of the people in the organizations. They might achieve some results, but these will be short-lived, and people in the organization will begin to dislike the environment.

Too many times, this conviction that work can be purposeful and effective is missing from organizations. As Farrakhan points out, "Bodies together in a room should not be assumed to be an organization."[14] Speaking to organizational development he says, "Organization only takes place when there is development of the individual as they are developed, they are manifested to the organizer who puts these individuals into a scheme or plan. These people start working together for the common good of the whole." The leader then becomes like a coach who is capable using the talents of the individuals in the organization to achieve a common goal. In the field of education, mission statements are supposed to guide the organization but are mostly only empty slogans. In part, this is because education driven by a human capitalist ideology sees students merely as future workers, causing schools and universities to reduce learning to data sets.

For Farrakhan, truth is the foundation for organization: "The Honorable Elijah Muhammad has made us to see and understand that truth is an organizing force of itself. This is why Jesus said, "You shall know the truth and the truth will set you free." Once you know the truth, then you know the value of organizing with and in accord with the truth. . . . And if you notice, the heavens are organized, the earth is organized, our bodies are organized. Why? Because inherent in truth is a principle of organization."[15] Scholars of organizational change echo Farrakhan's sentiments by exploring organizational change through the lens of biology and cosmology.

The educational leader should collaboratively organize vision around deep educational truths that give people a purpose for being in the organization. These educational truths will cause leadership expectations to be raised.

Believing in the Power of Conflict and Creativity

It is important to note that within organizations, there will be conflict in the organizing process. Leading during a climate of change is one of the difficulties of leadership. For educational leaders, the dynamic changes that are occurring at a rapid pace can be a source of conflict.

While most would look at conflict from a negative perspective, it could be argued that conflict brings out creativity. Conflict is typically related to hostility, and these hostilities might lead to personal attacks. This in turn creates toxic environments where there is no trust among the people in the organization. However, if we think of conflict as challenges that need solutions, conflicts become an opportunity for unleashing creativity—not just for the leaders but for all the staff and faculty and even students. It is the educational leader's role to ensure that conflict is seen as a creative opportunity and that it does not devolve into personal attacks or dislikes.

Believing in the Power of Diversity

A major challenge within educational institutions is the diversity that exists in them, which can result in constant change. As schools and colleges become more diverse, it will be important for educational leaders to understand how to organize this diversity. Farrakhan offers a powerful understanding of diversity and organization: "Or must you grow up to see the diversity in nature and the uniformity of God's great plan that all of us are not going to be the same? If you and I, recognizing our differences, cannot reach out to organize ourselves beyond our sameness, and to embrace that which is different from ourselves in the scheme of God's plan for own salvation, then we are always going to remain simple organizations that can never fully attain high goals."[16] There is a unity in diversity. And investing in diversity unleashes the gifts that each person possesses, which benefits everyone.

It is important for educational leaders to recognize the giftedness of people in the organization if they are to reach their full potential: "The Bible teaches us that God gives many gifts. We have one spirit but many gifts. Each one of us has a gift, which is related to the gift of everybody else. But these gifts mean nothing unless they are organized with a common goal and a common aim and purpose."[17]

Believing in the Power of Fun

Educational leaders should be striving to make school and universities places where fun exists. Apple writes, "Information which the children said they learned in school were all things that the teacher had told them during activities they called work. . . . First work includes any and all teacher-directed activities; only free-time activities were called play by the children."[18] Minister Farrakhan offers a compelling alternative to how schools currently operate:

> Fun is developing the creative mind that is seen in the sperm that has intelligence to seek the egg. A light of itself in a cell that rotates and revolves in the darkness of the womb that develops that which allows it to cling to the walls of the uterus on finding a firm resting place for growth that the body will not be able to expel this strange new life. . . . What is fun? Fun is watching intelligence develop. Fun is feeding intelligence to create the creative mind that the child will be able to say like God, Be and it is. That's fun.[19]

The development of the creative mind and the feeding of intelligence is education for leadership. If the student grows in the power to say "be and it is," it means that the student has the capacity to put in place certain organizing principles that were discussed earlier to bring an idea or ideas into reality. Once the idea becomes reality, the producer of that idea is catapulted into leadership.

Believing in the Power of Servanthood

Revisiting the idea of truth as an organizing principle implies that there is a need to shift from a profit-oriented view of organizations to one that has a servant view of leadership. In addition, educational leaders might consider thinking about schools and universities as serving organizations. The premise of serving organizations would align with Jesus's teaching that the greatest among you shall be your servant. Which brings us back to Greenleaf's defining characteristics of servant leadership: "1) natural feeling that one wants to serve, to serve first; and 2) Then conscious choice brings one to aspire to lead."[20]

In schools and universities, the concept of serving is lost in the current ideologies that are steeped in producing better workers. For educational leaders, service should extend to all of the persons in the organization. If we understand organizations as living organisms, it would be unwise for the head to diminish the toe. Too often, educational leaders do not value everyone in the organization, and, as Farrakhan points out, it's difficult to serve people if you feel as though they are beneath you. Farrakhan, speaking particularly to Black leadership, admonishes them to reflect on the quality of their hearts.

For Farrakhan, servant leadership also involves a commitment to challenging the status quo. Michael Dantley describes this type of leadership as *purposive leadership*, noting that "they are advocates of the tenets of critical pedagogy and promote its use in classrooms, particularly for African American students."[21] Farrakhan challenges leaders to reflect on leadership that in some ways may be doing the dirty work for those ruling the society. He challenges those in leadership positions to study scripture:

> Study the Book of John, Chapter 10. In Verse 8 Jesus said, "All that ever came before me were thieves and robbers..."; then in Verse 11 he gives a Principle of Leadership: "I am the good shepherd: the good shepherd giveth his life for the sheep." Evidently there were a lot of bad shepherds around. . . . "But he that is an hireling"—who's in it for the money; who's in it for the lust of power and influence— ". . . seeth the wolf coming, and leaveth the sheep, and fleeth: and the wolf catcheth them, and scattereth the sheep" (Verse 12). When "the wolf" comes, that kind of "hireling leadership" runs away. But the good shepherd will lay down his life for the sheep.[22]

In order to shift the leadership discourse, perhaps substituting the term *educational leader* with *minister* might bring about a change in how educational leaders enact their roles. Farrakhan, speaking to the etymology of the word *minister* through scriptural context, provides a new way of thinking about educational leadership:

> In the Book of Matthew, Chapter 20, verses 25–28: ". . . Jesus called them unto him, and said, Ye know that the princes of the Gentiles exercise dominion over them, and they that are great exercise authority upon them. But it shall not be so among you: but whosoever will be great among you, let him be your minister; And whosoever will be chief among you, let him be your servant . . ."—Boy! That's a heavy principle. Can you serve people that you think you're "better" than? Then Jesus said, "Even as the Son of man came not to be ministered unto, but to minister (unto others) . . ."—that means to "serve" others.[23]

Educational leaders performing as ministers are the model of servant leadership. The leader then becomes the minister serving the needs of the people. And through the attractive power of love, they lift and inspire the people to reach new levels of success. Moreover, they bring out of the people their unique talents and gifts.

CONCLUSION

Being a leader in the current educational climate is a difficult thing. The choice to lead must come from a burning desire to help others and "is based on serving, and seeing that the people whom you're serving value the service, benefit from the service and grow from the service; in order, then, that they become that to others as you have become that to them."[24] Leadership is the tapping of the divine essence within to the service of *doing good*.

Doing good requires that the leader use justice as the cornerstone for leadership. The conscious choice to lead does not come without a price. Because those in leadership roles become the targets of the problems, challenges, and issues that the organization may be confronted with. While facing these challenges, leaders may forget their aspirations to serve. Caught in the battles that come with leadership, the leader has to endure conflict and even attacks but should never have retaliatory spirit that causes them to act unjustly. Rising above emotions becomes paramount for educational leaders.

Farrakhan, in one of his study guides, "Rising above Emotions into the Thinking of God," writes, "The improper handling of Emotion does not allow us to grow beyond Self. It makes our reasoning subjective and clouds our judgment of individuals, circumstances and events. It makes us judge individuals, circumstances and events by how we are affected personally, thus we never see the bigger picture. Improper handling of Emotion makes us judge selfishly."[25] For those in leadership positions, the ability to see the bigger picture and do justice—despite the obstacles—is vital for the survival of the organization. So those in leadership roles must attend to rising above emotions that could make them become adversarial in their relationship with those under their leadership.

In these challenging times, leadership that is futuristic will be grounded in ideals that govern the creation. Concepts such as freedom, justice, and equality will be at the heart of those aspiring to leadership in the new world that is on the horizon. And while the current challenges facing educational leaders appear unmovable, there are universal laws at work that are bringing to birth a whole new reality. Leadership in the future will be grounded on the creative force that brought all things into existence—LOVE. And it is that behavior that must be practiced if schools, universities, and society are to enable their students to experience life on the highest plateau.

NOTES

1. Margaret J. Wheatley, *Finding Our Way: Leadership for an Uncertain Time* (San Francisco: Berrett-Koehler Publishers, 2005).
2. Wheatley, *Finding Our Way*, p. 2.
3. Louis Farrakhan, *A Torchlight for America* (Chicago, Final Call, 1993), p. 173.
4. Mwalimu J. Shujaa, ed., *Too Much Schooling, Too Little Education: A Paradox of Black Life in White Societies* (Trenton, NJ: Africa World Press, 1994).
5. Ivan Illich, *Deschooling Society* (New York: Harper & Row, 1971).
6. Wheatley, *Finding Our Way*.
7. Wheatley, *Finding Our Way*, p. 24.
8. Illich, *Deschooling Society*.
9. Wheatley, *Finding Our Way*, p. 19.
10. Donald L. Anderson, *Organizational Development: The Process of Leading Organizational Change* (Thousand Oaks, CA: Sage, 2015); W. Warner Burke, *Organizational Change: Theory and Practice* (Los Angeles: Sage, 2014).
11. Anderson. *Organizational Development*.
12. Douglas McGregor, *The Human Side of Enterprise* (New York: McGraw-Hill, 2006).
13. Thomas Starmack, *Organizational Behavior: A New Three Dimensional Leadership Paradigm* (San Diego: Cognella Academic Publishers, 2016), p. 31.
14. L. Farrakhan, "Truth, the Principle of Organization," *Final Call*, February 9, 2016.
15. Farrakhan, "Truth, the Principle of Organization."
16. Farrakhan, "Truth, the Principle of Organization."
17. Farrakhan, "Truth, the Principle of Organization."
18. Michael Apple, *Ideology and Curriculum* (New York: Routledge, 2004), p. 52.

19. Jabril Muhammad, *Closing the Gap: Inner Views of the Heart, Mind & Soul of the Honorable Minister Louis Farrakhan*, (Chicago, Final Call, 2009), p. 374.

20. Robert K. Greenleaf, *Servant Leadership: A Journey into the Nature of Legitimate Power and Greatness*, 25th anniversary edition. (New York: Paulist Press, 2002).

21. Michael Dantley, "African American Educational Leadership: Critical Purposive, and Spiritual," in *African American Perspectives on Leadership in Schools: Building a Culture of Empowerment*, ed. Lenoar Foster and Linda Tillman (Lanham, MD: Rowman & Littlefield Education, 2009).

22. Louis Farrakhan. "Principles and Practices of Leadership to Suffice Our Needs," *Final Call*, November 30, 2012.

23. Farrakhan, "Principles and Practices of Leadership to Suffice Our Needs."

24. Farrakhan, "Principles and Practices of Leadership to Suffice Our Needs."

25. Farrakhan, Self-Improvement Study Guides—Study Guide 18: "Rising Above Emotion Into the Thinking of God," The Farrakhan Factor (website), 1991, http://www.farrakhanfactor.com/clients/Factor/library/study_guides/studyguide_18.html.

Bibliography

Alexander, A. *The Farrakhan Factor: African American Writers on Leadership, Nationhood, and Minister Louis Farrakhan.* New York: Grove Press, 1998.

Allen, R. "The Race Problem in Critical Pedagogy Community." In *Reinventing Critical Pedagogy: Widening the Circle of Anti-Oppression Education*, edited by Ricky Allen and Marc Pruyn, pp. 3–21. Lanham, MD: Rowman & Littlefield, 2006.

Anderson, D. L. *Organizational Development: The Process of Leading Organizational Change.* Thousand Oaks, CA: Sage, 2015.

Anyon, J. "Social Class and the Hidden Curriculum of Work." *Journal of Education* 162, no. 1, 1980, 66–92.

Apple, M. *Ideology and Curriculum.* New York: Routledge, 2004.

Apple, M., W. Au, and L. Gandin, eds. *The Routledge International Handbook of Critical Education.* New York: Routledge, 2009.

Asante, M. K. *Race, Rhetoric, and Identity: The Architecton of Soul.* Amherst, NY: Humanity Books, 2005.

Banks, J. A. *An Introduction to Multicultural Education.* Upper Saddler River, NJ: Pearson, 2014.

Bell, D. *Faces at the Bottom of the Well: The Permanence of Racism.* New York: Basic Books, 1993.

Berliner, D., and B. Biddle. *The Manufactured Crisis: Myths, Fraud and the Attack on America's Public Schools.* New York: Addison Wesley, 1995.

Bowles, S., and H. Gintis. *Schooling in Capitalist America: Educational Reform and the Contradictions of Economic Life.* Chicago: Haymarket Books, 2011.

Bracey, G. *What You Should Know about the War against America's Public Schools.* New York: Allyn and Bacon, 2002.

Brookfield, S. *The Power of Critical Theory: Liberating Adult Learning and Teaching.* San Francisco: Jossey-Bass, 2005.

Burke, W. W. *Organizational Change: Theory and Practice.* Thousand Oaks, CA: Sage, 2014.

Chomsky, N. *Chomsky on Mis-Education.* Lanham, MD: Rowman & Littlefield, 2000.

Dantley, M. "African American Educational Leadership: Critical Purposive, and Spiritual." In *African American Perspectives on Leadership in Schools: Building a Culture of Empower-*

ment, edited by Lenoar Foster and Linda Tillman. Lanham, MD: Rowman & Littlefield Education, 2009.

Farrakhan, L. Self-Improvement Study Guides—"Self-Improvement: The Basis for Community Development." The Farrakhan Factor (website), 1991, http://www.farrakhanfactor.com/library/study_guides/self_improvement.html

Farrakhan, L. Self-Improvement Study Guides—Study Guide 3: "Overcoming Difficulty." The Farrakhan Factor (website), 1991, http://www.farrakhanfactor.com/library/study_guides/studyguide_03.html

Farrakhan, L. Self-Improvement Study Guides—Study Guide 18: "Rising Above Emotions Into the Thinking of God." The Farrakhan Factor (website), 1991, http://www.farrakhanfactor.com/clients/Factor/library/study_guides/studyguide_18.html.

Farrakhan, L. *Torchlight for America*. Chicago: Final Call, 1993.

Farrakhan, L. "Let Us Make a Man." Speech delivered April 11, 1994, Houston, Texas.

Farrakhan, L. "Louis Farrakhan Exposes Rothschild Bankers" [video]. Lecture delivered on Savior's Day, 1995, https://www.youtube.com/watch?v=_mAwjQpOalM

Farrakhan, L. *Education Is the Key*. Chicago: Final Call, 2006.

Farrakhan, L. *The Education Challenge: A New Educational Paradigm for the 21st Century*. Chicago: Final Call, 2009.

Farrakhan, L. "Principles and Practices of Leadership to Suffice Our Needs." *Final Call*, November 30, 2012.

Farrakhan, L. "The Life and Times of Muhammad Ali," lecture delivered June 12, 2016, at Mosque Maryam at the Nation of Islam's National Center in Chicago, https://www.noi.org/muhammad-ali/.

Farrakhan, L. "Truth, the Principle of Organization." Retrieved June 29, 2016 from http://www.finalcall.com/columns/mlf/mlf-organization.html.

Freire, P. *Pedagogy of the Oppressed*. New York: Continuum, 2000.

Fulani, L., and A. Sharpton. *Independent Black Leadership in America: Minister Louis Farrakhan, Dr. Lenora B. Fulani, Reverend Al Sharpton*. New York: Castillo International, 1993.

Gardell, M. *In the Name of Elijah Muhammad: Louis Farrakhan and The Nation of Islam*. Durham, NC: Duke University Press, 1996.

Gatto, J. T. *Dumbing Us Down: The Hidden Curriculum of Compulsory Schooling*. Gabriola Island, BC: New Society Publishers, 2005.

Gollnick, D., and P. Chinn. *Multicultural Education in a Pluralistic Society*, 9th ed. Boston: Pearson, 2013.

Greenleaf, R. K. *Servant Leadership: A Journey into the Nature of Legitimate Power and Greatness*. New York: Paulist Press, 1977.

Greenleaf, R. K. *Servant Leadership: A Journey into the Nature of Legitimate Power and Greatness*, 25th anniversary edition. New York: Paulist Press, 2002.

Hammond-Darling, L. "From 'Separate but Equal' to 'No Child Left Behind': The Collision of New Standards and Old Inequalities." In *Many Children Left Behind: How the No Child Left Behind Act Is Damaging Our Children and Our Schools*, edited by D. Meier and G. Woods, pp. 3–32. Boston: Beacon Press, 2004.

Hammond-Darling, L. "New Standards and Old Inequalities: School Reform and the Education of African American Students." In *Black Education: A Transformative Research and Action Agenda for the New Century*, edited by J. King, pp. 197–224. Mahwah, NJ: Lawrence Erlbaum Associates, 2005.

Hassan-EL, K. *The Willie Lynch Letter and the Making of Slaves*. Besenville, IL: Lushena Books, 2007.

Hilliard, A. *The Marron within Us: Selected Essays on African American Socialization.* Baltimore: Black Classic Press, 1995.
Hoyle, J. *Leadership and the Force of Love: Six Keys to Motivating People with Love.* Thousand Oaks, CA: Sage, 2002.
Hunter, J. *The Servant: A Simple Story about the True Essence of Leadership.* New York: Crown Publishing Group, 2012.
Illich, I. *Deschooling Society.* New York: Harper & Row, 1971.
Jacobson, R. R. *Pygmalion in the Classroom: Teacher Expectation and Pupils' Intellectual Development.* New York: Irvington Publishers, 1992.
Johnson, K., A. Pitre, and K. Johnson, eds. *African American Women Educators: A Critical Examination of Their Pedagogies, Educational Ideas, and Activism from the Nineteenth to the Mid-Twentieth Centuries.* Lanham, MD: Rowman & Littlefield Education, 2014.
King, J. E., ed. *Black Education: A Transformative Research and Action Agenda for the New Century.* Mahwah, NJ: Lawrence Erlbaum Associates, 2005.
Kozol, J. *Amazing Grace: The Lives of Children and the Conscience of a Nation.* New York: Crown, 1995.
Kozol, J. *Savage Inequalities: Children in America's Schools.* New York: HarperPerennial, 2012.
Kunjufu, K. *Black Students, Middle Class Teachers.* Chicago: African American Images, 2002.
Lipman, P. *Race and the Restructuring of School.* Albany: SUNY Press, 1998.
Marshall, C., and M. Oliva, eds., *Leadership for Social Justice: Making Revolutions in Education,* 2nd ed. Boston: Pearson, 2009.
Maxwell, J. C. *Developing the Leader within You.* Nashville: Thomas Nelson, 1993.
McLaren, P. *Life in Schools: An Introduction to Critical Pedagogy in the Foundations of Education,* 6th ed. Boulder, CO: Paradigm, 2015.
McLaren, P. *Pedagogy of Insurrections: From Resurrection to Revolution.* New York: Peter Lang, 2015.
McGregor, D. *The Human Side of Enterprise.* New York: McGraw-Hill, 2006.
Muhammad, E. *Message to the Blackman in America.* Chicago: Final Call, 1965.
Muhammad, J. *Closing the Gap: Inner Views of the Heart, Mind & Soul of the Honorable Minister Louis Farrakhan.* Chicago: Final Call, 2009.
Muhammad, K. "Making Our Community a Decent Place to Live Day." *Final Call,* March 30, 2016.
Muhammad, R. "Squashing 'Beefs' City by City with Conflict Resolution." *Final Call,* April 20, 2016.
Muhammad, R., E. Muhammad, and K. Muhammad. "Rebuilding The 'Hood.'" *Final Call,* April 12, 2016.
Nieto, S., and P. Bode. *Affirming Diversity: The Sociopolitical Context of Multicultural Education,* 6th ed. Boston: Allyn & Bacon, 2012.
Northouse, P. G. *Leadership: Theory and Practice.* Thousand Oaks, CA: Sage, 2016.
Oakes, J., and M. Lipton. *Teaching to Change the World,* 3rd ed. Boston: McGraw-Hill, 2007.
Pitre, A. *The Education Philosophy of Elijah Muhammad: Education for a New World,* 3rd ed. Lanham, MD: University Press of America, 2015.
Pitre, A., T. Allen, and E. Pitre, eds., *Multicultural Education for Educational Leaders: Critical Race Theory and Antiracist Perspectives.* Lanham, MD: Rowman & Littlefield, 2015.
Pitre, E. *Locked In: African American Males in Special Education.* New York: Linus Publication, 2011.
Rabaka, R. *Du Bois's Dialectics: Black Radical Politics and the Reconstruction of Critical Social Theory.* Lanham, MD: Lexington Books, 2008.

Rogers, C. *On Becoming a Person: A Therapist's View of Psychotherapy*. Boston: Houghton Mifflin, 1961.

Rosenthal, R., and L. Jacobson. *Pygmalion in the Classroom: Teacher Expectations and Pupils' Intellectual Development*. Wales, UK: Crown House Publishing, 1992.

Shields, C., ed. *Transformative Leadership: A Reader*. New York: Peter Lang, 2011.

Shor, I., and P. Freire. *A Pedagogy for Liberation: Dialogues on Transforming Education*. South Hadley, MA: Bergin & Garvey Publishers, 1987.

Shujaa, M. J., ed. *Too Much Schooling, Too Little Education: A Paradox of Black Life in White Societies*. Trenton, NJ: Africa World Press, 1994.

Singh, R. *The Farrakhan Phenomenon: Race, Reaction, and the Paranoid Style in American Politics*. Washington, DC: Georgetown University Press, 1997.

Sleeter, C., and C. Grant. *Making Choices for Multicultural Education: Five Approaches to Race, Class and Gender*. New York: Wiley, 2009.

Sleeter, C. "How White Teachers Construct Race." In *Race, Identity, and Representation in Education*, edited by Cameron McCarthy et al., pp. 243–56. New York: Routledge, 2005.

Spivey, D. *Schooling for the New Slavery: Black Industrial Education, 1868–1915*. Trenton, NJ: Africa World Press, 2007.

Spring, J. *American Education*. New York: McGraw-Hill, 2006.

Spring, J. *The Politics of American Education*. New York: Routledge, 2011.

Starmack, T. *Organizational Behavior: A New Three Dimensional Leadership Paradigm*. San Diego: Cognella Academic Publishers, 2016.

Strange, C. C., and J. Banning. *Educating By Design: Creating Campus Learning Environments That Work*. San Francisco: Jossey-Bass, 2001.

Theoharis, G., and M. Scanlan, eds. *Leadership for Increasingly Diverse Schools*. New York: Routledge, 2015.

Walker, D. *Islam and the Search for African American Nationhood: Elijah Muhammad, Louis Farrakhan, and the Nation of Islam*. Atlanta: Clarity Press, 2005.

Watkins, W. *The White Architects of Black Education: Ideology and Power in America 1865–1954*. New York: Teachers College Press, 2001.

Wheatley, M. J., *Finding Our Way: Leadership for an Uncertain Time*. San Francisco: Berrett-Koehler Publishers, 2005.

Woodson, C. G. *The Mis-Education of the Negro*. Drewryville, VA: Kha Books, 2008. Originally published Chicago: African American Images, 1933.

Zirin, D. "What to the Slave Is the Fourth of July." *The Nation*, July 4, 2012.

Index

additive approach, 2–3, 48
administrators, 23, 28
adversity, perseverance through, 36
African American studies, 47
alienation, 44–45
Anyon, Jean, 47
Apple, Michael, xxii, 2, 46, 58
athletes, Black, 43
authentic leadership, 20

banking model, of education, 2
Banks, James, 2, 5, 45–50
Banning, James, 29
Bible, 16, 25, 60
Black education: crisis in, ix; crossroads in, vii; historical background, viii; mis-education and, vii, xix–xx; White model for, 1–5
Black History Month, 41, 42
Black leaders, liberating education and, x
Blacks: athletes, 43; breaking process of enslaved, vii; criminalization of youth, 43; critical black pedagogy, xxii–xxiii, 41; dehumanizing of, vii; popular culture portrayal of, xx; in special education, 46
Block, Peter, 14
Bode, P., 48–49
Bowles, S., xxi
breaking process, vii
Brookfield, Stephen, 41–42, 44

Brown v. the Board of Education of Topeka, Kansas, viii, 42–43
"Business Is Warfare", 4

capitalism, xxi, 16
character, of leaders, 17–24; ego gratification and, 20, 27–28; empowerment and, 19, 24; humility in, 19–21; intelligence and, 23–24; perseverance quality in, 22–23; selflessness, 22, 24
Chinn, Phillip, 31–32
Chomsky, Noam, xix–xx
Civil War, viii
common-core curriculum, 47
conferences, critical pedagogy, xxii
conflict, creativity and, 57
contributions approach, 48
CORIBE, xi
Corinthians, 16
creativity, 55, 57
Creator, knowledge of, 6–7
criminality, 32, 43
critical black pedagogy, xxii–xxiii, 41
critical pedagogy, 39–41; conferences, xxii; *critical* in, xxii; early example of, 40; Farrakhan neglect by, xiv; ideology challenged by, 41–42; Woodson's foundational work in, 40, 41
critical White studies, 6

cultural deprivation theory, 8. *See also* popular culture
curriculum, 7, 46–48; common-core, 47; hidden, 47; of universities, 47–48

Dantley, Michael, 59
degrees, marketing of, 9–10
demonization, of Farrakhan, xxii
diversity, x, 48–49, 57–58
Divine Principle, 15
do-for-self actions, 30
domestication, education for, xx, 1–2
Douglass, Frederick, 40, 41

economic independence, 3–4
education: banking model of, 2; Black males in special, 46; Creator and, 6, 6–7; for domestication, xx, 1–2; dominant White model of, 1–5; Farrakhan's model of, 5–7; as leading out force, 10; liberating, x; new paradigm for, 54–55; purpose of, 5, 54; shadow system of, xxii; slavery as, 40; spiritual, 7–10; transformation through, 16–17; truths, 57–60; Wilson's prescription for, 46. *See also* Black education; leadership, educational; multicultural education; transformative educational leadership
educational scholarship, Farrakhan and, xiii
ego gratification, 20, 27–28
emergent leadership, 20
emotion, 60–61
empowerment, leadership and, 19, 24
entertainment world, 43
expectations, teacher, 8

Farrakhan, Louis, x; "Business Is Warfare" speech of, 4; demonization of, xxii; educational leadership role of, xiv; education model of, 5–7; love defined by, 17; neglect of, xiv; people taught by, 24; on principles and daily life, 28; as problematic, xxiii; summary of ideas and works, xxiii–xxiv. *See also specific topics*
forgiveness, 18–19
Frankfurt School, xxii, 40

Freire, Paulo, xxiii, 2, 34, 43
Fruit of Islam, 31
fun, 58
futuristic leadership, 53–61; challenges for, 53–54; emotions and, 60–61; love and, 61; new paradigm for, 54–55; organizations in, 55–60

Gandhi, Mohandas, 24
gang leaders, 32–33
Garvey, Marcus, x
Gatto, John Taylor, 6
Georgia, "Bluff" area of, 30
Gintis, H., xxi
God, 55, 57–58, 60; consciousness, 8; leadership as starting with, 25; Solomon and, 25. *See also* Creator
Gollnick, Donna, 31–32
Greenleaf, Robert, 27, 59

Harvard Civil Rights Project, ix
hegemony, xx, xxi, 42
hidden curriculum, 47
Hoover, J. Edgar, 44
Hoyle, John, 14, 18
human motivation theory, 56
human needs, 28; belonging and love, 32–34; food, water, and shelter, 29–31; safety and security, 31–32; self-actualization, 35–36; self-esteem, 34–35
humility, 19–21

ideologies, transformative leadership as challenging, 41–42
Illich, Ivan, 54, 55
influence: gang leader, 32–33; leadership as, 13; position and, 34
inner-city schools, 29
intelligence, leadership and, 23–24
interest-convergence, 42–43
IQ, 8
Islam. *See* Nation of Islam

jails, 43
Jesus, 9, 17, 20–21, 30, 59

King, Joyce, xi
King, Martin Luther, Jr., 24, 40

knowledge: of Creator, 6, 7; liberatory, xiv; love of, 24; of self, 6–8; self-actualization and, 36; thirst for, 8; as worth and potential, 23
Kozol, Jonathan, 29

leaders: critical black pedagogy and, 41; forgiveness in, 18–19; gang, 32–33; as ministers, 59–60; as teachers, 23
leadership, educational: authentic, 20; challenge facing today's, 13; cloud analogy, 16–17; community needs and, 29–31; Divine Principle for, 15; emergent, 20; Farrakhan role in, xiv; as influence, 13; listening and, 21–22, 24; as love, 15–17; management *vs.*, 14–16; minister replacing leader, 59–60; price of, 60; purposive, 59; relationship-building, 15; scripture study in, 59; traditional concept of, 28; transactional, 16; transformational differentiated from transformative, 39; transformative, 39–50. *See also* character, of leaders; futuristic leadership; organizations, in futuristic leadership; servant leadership; transformative educational leadership
liberating education, x
liberatory knowledge, xiv
"The Life and Times of Muhammad Ali" (Farrakhan), 41
listening, leadership characteristic, 21–22, 24
love: belonging and, 32–34; empowerment through, 19; Farrakhan's definition of, 17; forgiveness and, 18–19; futuristic leadership and, 61; humility and, 19–21; of knowledge, 24; leadership as, 15–17; perseverance and, 23

Malcolm X, xxi, 6, 8
management: leadership *vs.*, 14–16; middle-, 28
Mandela, Nelson, 24
marketing, of degrees, 9–10
Maslow, Abraham, 28, 31, 33, 35
Maxwell, John, 13
McGregor, D., 56
McLaren, Peter, xx, xxi, 9

A Message to the Blackman in America (Muhammad, E.), 3, 40
middle-management, 28
Million Man March, x–xi, xiii, 44
ministers, educational leaders as, 59–60
mis-education, vii, xix–xx
mistakes, 18
Mother Theresa, 24
Muhammad, Elijah, vii, x, xiv, 3, 8, 15; critical pedagogy of, 40; economics saving plan of, 4; knowledge of God taught by, 6; on ruling elite, xx–xxi; on slavemasters and education, 48; table talks of, 21
Muhammad, Willie, 32
Muhammad University of Islam, 7, 41
multicultural education, 2–3, 5, 6; Banks multicultural reform approaches, 48; benchmarks of transformative educational leadership and, 45–50; policy statement, 45–46
Multicultural Education in a Pluralistic Society (Chinn and Gollnick), 31–32
Muslim Girls Training Class, 31

Nation of Islam, xi; belonging and love practiced in, 33; criticism of, 41; do-for-self actions of, 30; economic independence idea in, 3–4; God consciousness expectation of, 8; self-defense classes, 31; on self-esteem, 34; university course on, 47
needs. *See* human needs
Nieto, S., 48–49
No Child Left Behind Act, vii–viii, ix–x, xxi
Northouse, Peter G., xxiii, 13, 20

oppressed, unity of, 44
organizations, in futuristic leadership, 55–60; diversity and, 57–58; mechanizing problem, 55; organizing principle, 57; power of fun in, 58; power of purpose in, 56–57; servanthood and, 59–60

parent participation, 49–50
pedagogy. *See* critical black pedagogy; critical pedagogy

perseverance, 22–23, 36
philosophy, meaning of word, 24
play time, 24
popular culture, xx
position, influence and, 34
professional development, 45–46
propaganda, xix
purposive leadership, 59
Pygmalion effect, 8

Race to the Top, vii–viii, xxi
relationship-building, 15
ruling elites, viii, xix–xxi; domesticating agenda of, xx

safety and security, 31–32
schools and school system: Anyon on types of, 47; campus design and, 29; after Civil War, viii; Kozol's study of inner-city, 29; mechanizing, 55; Muhammad University of Islam, 7, 41; rebuilding of, 30; ruling elites as controlling, viii, xix; safety in, 31–32; staff, 49; tracking, viii, ix
scripture study, 59
second-generation segregation, viii
secretary, first day of, 18
segregation, viii, ix
self-actualization, 35–36
self-defense training, 31
self-esteem, 34–35, 46
"Self-Improvement—The Basis for Community" Development" (Farrakhan), 35
self-knowledge, 6–8
selflessness in leadership, 22, 24
self-organizing processes, 53, 54
servant leadership: belonging and love needs, 32–34; concept and definition, 27–28; food, water, and shelter needs and, 29–31; safety and security needs and, 31–32; self-actualization and, 27–37; self-esteem and, 34–35; servanthood power in organizations, 59–60
Shabazz, Abdulalim, 8
shadow education system, xxii
Shields, Carolyn, 39
Shujaa, Mwalimu, 54

slavemasters, 3, 48
slavery, 7, 40; breaking process of, vii
social action approach, 48
"Social Class and the Hidden Curriculum of Work" (Anyon), 47
social reproduction theory, xxi
Socrates, 5
Solomon, God and, 25
special education, 46
spiritual education, 7–10
sports, 43
Spring, Joel, xxi, 46
Starmack, T., 56
Strange, Charles, 29
street life, 14

table talks, 21, 22
teachers: expectations of, 8; leaders as, 23; in spiritual education, 7–10
teacher within, 7
teaching materials, 50
teaching strategies, 48–49
thirst, for knowledge, 8
tracking, segregation and, viii, ix
transactional leadership, 16
transformation, 16–17; Banks approach, 48
transformative educational leadership: Banks' multicultural reforms, 48; benchmarks of, 45–50; challenges for future, 50; curriculum and, 46–48; multicultural education policy statement, 45–46; parent participation, 49–50; school staff and, 49; staff attitudes and, 46; teaching materials and, 50; teaching strategies, 48–49
transformative leadership, 39–50; alienation overcome by, 44–45; black leaders on critical pedagogy, 41; as critical pedagogy, 39–41; definition of, 39; ideologies challenged by, 41–42; power unmasked by, 42–44; transformational distinguished from, 39
truths: educational, 57–60; organization foundation as, 57; power of diversity, 57–58

unity, of oppressed, 44
universities, curriculum of, 47–48

vandalism, 31
vices, 4
violence, 43

Walmart, xxi
Watkins, William, xix

Wheatley, Margaret, 53, 54
White model of education, 1–5
White studies, 6
White supremacy, 4–6, 40–42
Wilson, Woodrow, 46
Woodson, Carter G., viii, x, xix, 40, 41

About the Author

Abul Pitre is professor of educational leadership at Prairie View A&M University, where he teaches courses in multicultural education and leadership. He was appointed Edinboro University's first named professor for his outstanding work in African American education and held the distinguished title of the Carter G. Woodson Professor of Education.

www.ingramcontent.com/pod-product-compliance
Lightning Source LLC
Chambersburg PA
CBHW020753230426
43665CB00009B/580